SEASONS
—— *of* ——
SUFFERING
—— *and* ——
SUCCESS

PATRICK M. MORLEY

LIFEWAY PRESS
Nashville, Tennessee

© Copyright 1996 • Patrick Morley
Reprinted December 2002
All rights reserved

No part of this book may be reproduced or transmitted in any form or by any
means, electronic or mechanical, including photocopying and recording, or by any
information storage or retrieval system, except as may be expressly permitted in
writing by the publisher. Requests for permission should be addressed in writing to
LifeWay Press; One LifeWay Plaza; Nashville, TN 37234-0175

ISBN 0-8054-9785-4

This book is a resource in the Personal Life category of the
Christian Growth Study Plan. Course CG–0180
Dewey Decimal Classification: 248.842
Subject Heading: MEN–RELIGIOUS LIFE

Acknowledgements
The Curriculum Products are based on *The Seven Seasons of a Man's Life*, by Patrick
Morley, and created under license granted by Thomas Nelson, Inc.
Unless otherwise indicated, Scripture quotations are from the Holy Bible,
New International Version, copyright © 1973,1978,1984, by International Bible Society
Scripture quotations marked NKJV are from the *New King James Version*.
Copyright © 1979, 1980, 1982, Thomas Nelson, Inc., Publishers.
Scripture quotations marked TLB are taken from *The Living Bible*. Copyright ©
Tyndale House Publishers, Wheaton, Illinois, 1971. Used by permission.

Design: Edward Crawford   Cover Illustration: Michael Schwab
Curriculum Writer: Larry Keefauver   Coordinating Editor: David Delk

Order additional copies of this book by writing to Customer Service Center, One
LifeWay Plaza; Nashville, TN 37234-0113; by calling toll free (800) 458-2772; by
faxing (615) 251-5933; by ordering online at *www.lifeway.com*; by emailing *customerservice@lifeway.com*; or by visiting a LifeWay Christian Store.

Printed in the United States of America

Leadership and Adult Publishing
LifeWay Church Resources
One LifeWay Plaza
Nashville, TN 37234-0175

CONTENTS

INTRODUCTION

WELCOME to The Seasons of Suffering and Success. Each man experiences times of suffering and times of success. These seasons call men to reflect on the meaning and purpose of life and to build life on sure foundations. I want you to know...

You are not alone. I have discovered that every man experiences seven seasons during his life.

 The Season of Reflection

 The Season of Building

 The Season of Crisis

 The Season of Renewal

 The Season of Rebuilding

 The Season of Suffering

 The Season of Success

I have prepared four books in this collection to help you explore these seasons. This book focuses on the seasons of suffering and success.

Each week during the next six weeks you will have five daily studies to read and complete. You will need 20 to 30 minutes each day.

Each day a BIG IDEA will be presented. The BIG IDEA (identified with this symbol ◆) captures the main point for that day's lesson in one sentence. The rest of the material for that day amplifies, expands, explains, and applies the BIG IDEA.

You will also read other statements with which you will highly identify. Let me encourage you to underline, make notes, and write down questions about ideas you don't agree with or understand. If you are studying with a group, bring up your questions with the other men.

For added review, a list of key ideas called *The Bottom Line* appears at the end of each day's lesson.

Let me urge you to find a group of men to study with you. Use the Leader Guide on pages 126-139. This investment will bring a great return.

You and your spiritual pilgrimage are the focal point of this study. The subject is God and wisdom to live under His authority and grace. So, in each lesson you will be encouraged to apply the truths and principles to your life situation.

I pray that God will use this study in a wonderful and powerful way in your life. Millions of men are experiencing a hunger for God. They want to think more deeply about their lives. They are seeking to become the spiritual leaders of their homes and discover God's will for their lives. Whichever season of life you find yourself in, this study will encourage you to keep going.

Would you like to learn more about the ministry of Patrick Morley? Partnering with churches and ministries, our vision is to reach every man in America with compelling opportunities to be transformed by Jesus Christ. Our strategies include:
• Man in the Mirror Seminars
• The Man in the Mirror Leadership Institute
• Publishing Christian literature
• Serving churches and other ministries
• TGIF Men's Ministry in Orlando, Florida
If you would like to receive 3 sample issues of our monthly newsletter for men, send your name and address to:

Patrick Morley Ministries
180 Wilshire Blvd.
Casselberry, FL 32707

LIFE'S SEASONS

There is a time for everything,
and a season for every activity
   under heaven:
a time to be born and a time to die,
a time to plant and a time to uproot,
a time to kill and a time to heal,
a time to tear down and a time to build,
a time to weep and a time to laugh,
a time to mourn and a time to dance,
a time to scatter stones and a time to
   gather them,
a time to embrace and a time to refrain,
a time to search and a time to give up,
a time to keep and a time to throw away,
a time to tear and a time to mend,
a time to be silent and a time to speak,
a time to love and a time to hate,
a time for war and a time for peace.

                    –Ecclesiastes 3:1-8

The Season
of Suffering

THE NATURE OF SUFFERING

In his younger days Ken, a developer, builder, and pilot, was by his own admission a high flier. He didn't marry until he turned 32. He prayed and asked God to give him a son. The Lord answered his prayer, but his son was brain-damaged. He accepted the news and began to investigate how to raise him best. Many of his friends said, however, "Don't waste your life on that boy."

"But he's my son. He's of my own flesh." Ken found a specialized school in Orlando and moved his family there from Jacksonville. He commuted back and forth for five years, leaving Orlando each Monday morning and returning Friday evening until he was able to move his business.

Under the loving tutelage of devoted teachers, young Tommy learned how to read and write. Eventually, he graduated from the University of Central Florida. Turns out Tommy is a computer whiz, and today he manages the computer system for a privately-owned student dormitory.

I asked Ken, "What would you say to those people today who told you, 'Don't waste your life on that boy'?"

After a long, thoughtful pause, he said, "I wouldn't trade this for anything. I thought I was a real mover and shaker. It's as though the Lord wanted me to see there is another world out there.

"Tommy has taught us how to love, and he has taught us about miracles. My wife, Susan, put it this way, 'God, I am so glad I didn't miss this!' Tommy truly is a joy to Susan.

"When Tommy was growing up, he couldn't understand why girls didn't like him. He has weak eyes—he has to be driven everywhere—and he's not very tall.

"When he was growing up, he would sit around the house and ask, 'Why doesn't anybody ever call me? Why doesn't anyone ever want to do anything with me?'

"This would break our hearts. When he would talk like this, which was often, Susan and I would both become quiet. Each knew what the other was doing. We were praying for God to give Tommy a friend.

"Many, many times within five minutes the phone would ring for Tommy, and someone would say he wanted to come by or go to a movie or something like that. This is how we learned about miracles."

We all face periods of suffering in our lives. They may not be as involved as Ken's situation. Nevertheless, they occur. For the next two weeks, we will explore the Season of Suffering. We will raise many questions as we seek to understand:

• The nature of suffering
• Four consoling truths about suffering

★ DAY 1 ★ The Questions Suffering Raises	★ DAY 2 ★ The Character of God	★ DAY 3 ★ Is Suffering Good or Bad?

★ DAY 4 ★ Three Ways We Suffer	★ DAY 5 ★ The Gift of Suffering

Our response to suffering, discipline, hardships, and trials determines how much we grow and mature spiritually. Memorize and meditate on these verses during the coming week.

> I know what it is to be in need, and I know what it is to have plenty. I have learned the secret of being content in any and every situation, whether well fed or hungry, whether living in plenty or in want. I can do everything through him who gives me strength (Philippians 4:12-13).

It is my prayer that these two weeks on the Season of Suffering will be a significant period of growth, insight, and drawing near to God.

THE QUESTIONS
SUFFERING RAISES

What is suffering? Is what we call suffering really suffering? There can be no question that what Ken, Susan, and their son Tommy have had to live through has brought sorrow. Yet, when measured against the great good that has resulted, who is to say?

Write your definition of suffering. Cite an example from your life to illustrate your definition.

_____

_____

Keep your definition in mind as you study. Perhaps during the next few weeks God will lead you to fine-tune your definition.

When we look around, we see a lot of suffering in the world. Place a check beside types of suffering that you have recently read about in the newspaper or heard about on radio or TV.

_____ Natural disasters (storms, earthquakes, etc.)
_____ Freedoms taken away through force
_____ Persecution and martyrdom of Christians
_____ Famine and extreme poverty
_____ Wars
_____ Abandoned and orphaned children
_____ Physical diseases
_____ Emotional or psychological illness

I don't know about you, but when I look over such a list and add my own particular perspectives on suffering, I am overwhelmed by sadness and questions. We have all agonized over the question, "Why do bad things happen to good or innocent people?"

Perhaps we have agonized even more over the question, "Why do bad things happen to *me*?"

◆

Suffering makes us face the deepest questions about our lives.

What are some of the recurring questions you have about suffering? Here's my list. Check the questions that cause you to struggle most.
❑ Exactly what is suffering?
❑ Why do innocent people suffer?
❑ Is suffering inevitable?
❑ What causes suffering?
❑ Why does there have to be suffering at all?

Does the suffering you've witnessed or endured cause you to question God's character?   ❑ yes   ❑ no   ❑ not sure.

If you answered *yes,* you're certainly not alone. For most people, the issue comes down to two questions:
• If God is *good,* why does He allow situations that cause people to suffer?
• If God is *all-powerful,* why doesn't He remove all suffering?

These questions lead us to what philosophers and theologians call the problem of evil. Respected Christian philosopher Alvin Plantinga has said that the most impressive argument of the atheist has to do with the problem of evil.[1]

David Hume framed the problem well when he wrote, "Epicurus's old questions are yet unanswered. Is He (God) willing to prevent evil, but not able? Then He is impotent. Is He able, but not willing? Then He is malevolent. Is He both able and willing? Whence then is evil?"[2]

Humanly speaking, the implications about our sufferings are that:
1. God doesn't know (*ignorance,* He is not *all-knowing*).
2. God can't do anything about it (*impotence,* He is not *all-powerful*).
3. God doesn't care (*malevolence,* He is not *all-good*).

Either God is sovereign or He's not, and either God is good or He's not. Is God sovereign? All-powerful? Is God in control of all things? The unequivocal claim of Scripture is yes. Is God good? All-benevolent? Committed to our good? The unequivocal claim of Scripture is yes. Can we fully understand how God is in complete control and completely good? No, we cannot. But we can trust Him. God works for our good. Tomorrow we will illustrate this more fully.

Read the following passages. Circle which of God's characteristics are revealed.

"When Abram was ninety-nine years old, the Lord appeared to him and said, 'I am God Almighty; walk before me and be blameless' " (Genesis 17:1).

Almighty   Good   In control   Committed to our good

"You are good, and what you do is good; teach me your decrees" (Psalm 119:68).

Almighty   Good   In control   Committed to our good

"I know that the Lord is great, that our Lord is greater than all gods. The Lord does whatever pleases him, in the heavens and on the earth, in the seas and all their depths" (Psalm 135:5-6).

Almighty   Good   In control   Committed to our good

"We know that in all things God works for the good of those who love him, who have been called according to his purpose" (Romans 8:28).

Almighty   Good   In control   Committed to our good

From these Scriptures, we see that God is almighty, good, in control, and committed to our good. That's God's nature.

Think of the times you have endured suffering. What have you learned about God in those times? What have you learned about yourself? What can you share with others that will help them? As you study this week, keep these questions in mind. Remember the goodness and faithfulness, and be able to share with others what you have learned through suffering.

Review today's lesson. What one Scripture passage was most meaningful to you? Write it below.

_____

_____

Write a prayer asking for God's wisdom and guidance in understanding and sharing about suffering.

_____

_____

The Bottom Line
* Suffering makes us face the deepest questions about our lives.
* God is in complete control, and He is completely good.

---

[1]Alvin Plantinga, *God and Other Minds* (Ithaca: Cornell University Press, 1966), 115.

[2]David Hume, *God and the Problem of Evil*, from *Dialogues Concerning Natural Religion*, in William L. Rowe and William J. Wainwright, eds., *Philosophy of Religion: Selected Readings* (New York: Harcourt Brace Jovanovich, 1973), 187.

THE CHARACTER OF GOD

Two days before she was to arrive home from college for Thanksgiving break, our freshman daughter phoned.

We had missed her deeply, and like many of her classmates, she was really getting homesick. When she phoned this particular Sunday night, she was suffering. She wept as she told how she had less than four dollars in cash and didn't know how she was going to get home.

She was also going through some culture shock that had her feeling down. She was used to warm, hugging, joking-around relationships with all the kids, both boys and girls, at the small Christian high school from which she graduated.

To top things off, she had two papers due and a major exam to study for, all of which when added together had her totally stressed out.

Money problems. Social problems. School problems. All in all, it pushed her into overload. My wife, Patsy, listened on one extension of the phone and I on another. As our daughter talked and occasionally broke down, my breathing became labored, and my heart felt like it was breaking. More than anything else in the whole world, I wanted to reach out, wave a magic wand, and make every problem go away. Yet, I also knew that would be exactly the wrong thing to do.

We encouraged her, mostly by listening, and agreed how good it would be to see each other. Her mother explained how to charge gas and food for the 10-hour drive home with the credit card we had given her for emergencies. As Patsy and I hung up the phone, I had to brush tears from the corners of my eyes.

Patsy and I talked the situation over, and we agreed: The worst possible thing we could have done for our beloved daughter would have been to rescue her from her problems. *Truly loving parents have goals for their children that are larger than their immediate sufferings.*

We love our daughter more than life itself, and would do anything possible to make her life easier unless in the end it would make her life harder. But we knew that her circumstances, as hard as they appeared, would result in a greater good in the long run.

We allowed her to suffer so she could grow, become strong in character, develop discipline, learn responsibility, gain confidence, learn to trust God more, and in the end, be a better person. For her own good we disciplined her, as we thought best, by not rescuing her. That's how God operates with us; that's the character of God.

◆

God never allows any suffering, pain, or evil to touch us unless it will bring about a greater good or prevent a greater evil.

Recall a time in your life when God did not immediately rescue you from pain or circumstances. Briefly describe what you learned and how you grew in character.

_____

_____

_____

Pain is often God's warning system. A few days ago I bumped my knee on my desk, and it really hurt. The knee is a sensitive, important part of my body. God invented "bump pain" to warn us that harder blows will create even more pain. Bump pain teaches us to be more careful. Bump pain protects us from greater harm. The pain of an argument with your wife is a warning system to settle things with her so a greater calamity doesn't happen later.

Check the "bump pains" you have experienced in recent weeks.
❑ Overdrawn checking account
❑ Correction or criticism by someone you respect
❑ Argument or correction from your wife
❑ Withdrawal by a child
❑ Credit rejection
❑ Less than positive evaluation at work
❑ Speeding ticket
❑ Moodiness or outbursts of anger
❑ Other: _____

THE SEASONS OF SUFFERING AND SUCCESS

Bump pains could be an early warning sign God is using to correct us before more serious problems arise. Describe what God may be doing in your life through one of the bump pains you recently experienced.

_____

_____

As our Heavenly Father, God loves us enough to put the development of our character before the development of our circumstances. He will always add to your suffering the necessary ingredients to turn it into a blessing, even if it takes a period of time. The suffering God allows is never for your harm, but always for your well-being.

Each circumstance produces a maturing effect in our lives, leading us from suffering to perseverance to character to hope (see Romans 5:3-5)—pointing us to the knowledge of God's deep and abiding love for us.

God corrects us because He loves us. Read the following passage and circle words or phrases you have experienced in your life.

"My son, do not make light of the Lord's discipline,
    and do not lose heart when he rebukes you,
because the Lord disciplines those he loves,
    and he punishes everyone he accepts as a son."

Endure hardship as discipline; God is treating you as sons. For what son is not disciplined by his father? If you are not disciplined (and everyone undergoes discipline), then you are illegitimate children and not true sons. Moreover, we have all had human fathers who disciplined us and we respected them for it. How much more should we submit to the Father of our spirits and live! Our fathers disciplined us for a little while as they thought best; but God disciplines us for our good, that we may share in his holiness. No discipline seems pleasant at the time, but painful. Later on, however, it produces a harvest of righteousness and peace for those who have been trained by it (Hebrews 12:5-11).

As God's children, we need His discipline. We need the suffering He allows to build and strengthen our character. As we become able to endure and overcome difficulties, we become more effective witnesses to His power at work in us.

 What does God want you to do as a result of today's study?

The Bottom Line
- Truly loving parents have goals for their children that are larger than their immediate sufferings.
- God never allows any suffering, pain, or evil to touch us unless it will bring about a greater good or prevent a greater evil.
- Pain is often God's warning system.
- God invented "bump pain" to warn us that harder blows will create even more pain.
- As our Heavenly Father, God loves us enough to put the development of our character before the development of our circumstances.
- As God's children, we need His discipline.

IS SUFFERING GOOD OR BAD?

Once upon a time a farmer captured a wild stallion. His neighbor said to him, "Sure glad to hear your good news."

The farmer replied, "Good news, bad news, who knows?"

A few days later the farmer's son asked if he could break in the horse. The stallion threw him off, and he broke his leg.

The farmer's neighbor said, "Sorry to hear your bad news."

The farmer replied, "Good news, bad news, who knows?"

A week later war broke out, and all the young men in the city were drafted to go off to fight.

The neighbor leaned across the fence and said, "Sure turned out to be good news, the way your boy broke his leg and all."

The farmer replied, "Good news, bad news, who knows?"

We do not see the larger picture of what God is doing in the world. Things that appear to be suffering and hardship, biblically speaking, form the ingredients of greater goods and the means to prevent greater evils.

◆

God uses every circumstance to help us mature, develop, and grow.

God does not author evil nor will it. God overcomes evil. Eventually, we see His Hand at work in every circumstance. Think of a time in your life that was from your perspective "bad news." Briefly describe how God worked in you and your situation to produce "good news."

_____

_____

_____

God actually uses suffering and hardship for our eternal good. Suffering is redeemed through the power of Almighty God. Consider the Old Testament character Joseph. Genesis 37 tells how Joseph's brothers sold him to slave traders who took him far away to Egypt. Genesis 39 tells how Joseph was falsely accused of sexual harassment and was thrown into prison. Eventually, through God's miraculous intervention, Joseph was released from prison and rose to be second in command in all of Egypt. When his brothers came to him for food in a time of famine, Joseph had the opportunity to "get even." But he chose not to. Genesis 50:19-20 tells why. Look up that passage and record it on the lines provided.

_____

_____

Certainly, the same God who redeemed Joseph's suffering can redeem ours as well. Read the following passages and underline how God brings redemption from suffering.

For the creation was subjected to frustration, not by its own choice, but by the will of the one who subjected it, in hope that the creation itself will be liberated from its bondage to decay and brought into the glorious freedom of the children of God (Romans 8:20-21).

But he (the Lord) said to me, "My grace is sufficient for you, for my power is made perfect in weakness." Therefore I will boast all the more gladly about my weaknesses, so that Christ's power may rest on me. That is why, for Christ's sake, I delight in weaknesses, in insults, in hardships, in persecutions, in difficulties. For when I am weak, then I am strong (2 Corinthians 12:9-10).

We should be cautious about thinking of our hardships as hardships. Rather, what we often think of as suffering is really the means of grace to bring us into a closer reliance upon God.

Certainly I'm not saying our sufferings don't hurt. I'm not suggesting the pain is not real. Rather, they are minimal compared to the benefits they achieve for us. Why does a bodybuilder endure pain until his muscles groan for rest? He does so because he knows it is the only way he can achieve his goal. In the same way, the Bible says that "our light and momentary troubles are achieving for us an eternal glory that far outweighs them all" (2 Corinthians 4:17).

Can you think of a time in your life when God used a hardship to bring you closer to Him?

_____

Truly, we serve a great God. He is not only able to start with nothing and create something good, but God is also able to start with something bad and make it good. Close today by writing a brief prayer thanking God for His loving interest in your life and His willingness and ability to redeem your suffering.

_____

_____

_____

The Bottom Line
- God uses every circumstance to help us mature, develop, and grow.
- What we often think of as suffering is really the means of grace to bring us into a closer reliance upon God.

THREE WAYS
WE SUFFER

Here's what real suffering is: To be allowed to completely direct our own lives to our eventual destruction. Tragic suffering results when we rebel and abandon the chastening that comes from a loving Heavenly Father.

We do not know what a day may bring forth, but we do know who brings forth the day. God is a God of purpose. He is working out everything in conformity to the purpose of His will. What men mean for harm, God means for good, for the saving of many lives. God even uses the evil men perpetrate upon us for good.

We may suffer one of three ways: (1) for doing wrong, (2) for doing right, or (3) for no apparent reason. How we respond to our suffering depends on why we are suffering in the first place.

◆

The wise man will look beyond his suffering to the reasons for it.

Are we suffering the consequences of a wrong decision? Or are we suffering because we stood for what is right?

When you are suffering God's correction and the consequences of a wrong done, how do you respond? Check your usual responses.

❑ Anger ❑ Determination not to do that wrong again
❑ Depression ❑ Desire to learn from God
❑ Self-Pity ❑ Desire to get beyond correction to restoration
❑ Frustration ❑ Impatience
❑ Hurt ❑ Humbleness before God
❑ Pain ❑ Anxiety or worry

If we are suffering the consequences of a wrong decision and God is chastening and correcting, we must submit to the blows of His loving correction. On the other hand, if we are going through a season of suffering because we stood up for right, we can be glad. Our response may vary.

Read the Scriptures below and circle words or phrases that describe how we can respond when we suffer for His name's sake.

"Blessed are you when people insult you, persecute you and falsely say all kinds of evil against you because of me. Rejoice and be glad, because great is your reward in heaven, for in the same way they persecuted the prophets who were before you" (Matthew 5:11-12).

Dear friends, do not be surprised at the painful trial you are suffering, as though something strange were happening to you. But rejoice that you participate in the sufferings of Christ, so that you may be overjoyed when his glory is revealed (1 Peter 4:12-15).

What brings about persecution from others for His name's sake? At times, Christians are persecuted because they are not sensitive to those around them. But there are times when Christians must stand up for right and be persecuted. Such was the case in Nazi Germany for Christians like Dietrich Bonhoeffer who resisted German persecution of the Jews. Such resisters were imprisoned and often killed.

What are some issues for which you would risk persecution or even death for the cause of Christ? List two or three things you would be willing to do to stand for Christ.

_____

_____

Many times, however, we don't have a clue about why we are going through various trials and temptations. Our sufferings seem to be without reason or logic. It is as though we are standing around minding our own business and all of a sudden, "life" happens. Perhaps the hardest sufferings to understand are the seemingly random acts of pain that befall us all from time to time. In such situations we must submit ourselves to the mercy of God and continue to do good.

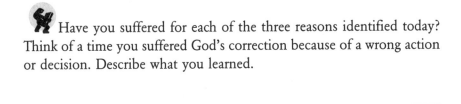 Have you suffered for each of the three reasons identified today? Think of a time you suffered God's correction because of a wrong action or decision. Describe what you learned.

Think of a time you suffered persecution for Christ. Describe how He saw you through.

Think of a time you experienced random suffering that happened without apparent reason. How did you respond?

Based on what you've learned so far in this book and from personal Bible study, how will you respond to suffering in the future?

The Bottom Line
- Here's what real suffering is: To be allowed to completely direct our own lives to our eventual destruction.
- The wise man will look beyond his suffering to the reasons for it.
- Many times we don't have a clue about why we are going through various trials and temptations.
- In such situations we must submit ourselves to the mercy of God and continue to do good.

THE GIFT
OF SUFFERING

An American Christian and a Chinese Christian were speaking to each other. The American said, "I've always wondered, if God loves the Chinese people, why does He let them suffer?"

"That's interesting," replied the Chinese believer. "I've always wondered, if God loves the American people, why doesn't He let them suffer?"

 What do you suppose this Chinese brother gained from his suffering that enabled him to see it as an expression of God's love? Of course, we can't know for sure without asking him, but write your hypothesis here.

_____

_____

The suffering represented by the cross of Christ is redemptive. God can redeem your time of suffering through the cross. In the cross below, describe a time when your suffering was redeemed as God used it to teach you an important lesson.

◆

Suffering is not just a test, it is also a blessing.

When suffering, whether ours or someone else's, touches our lives, our faith grows. Read the following Scripture, then write on the lines below the purposes of suffering.

"In this you greatly rejoice, though now for a little while you may have had to suffer grief in all kinds of trials. These have come so that your faith—of greater worth than gold, which perishes even though re-fined by fire—may be proved genuine and may result in praise, glory and honor when Jesus Christ is revealed" (1 Peter 1:6-7).

_____

_____

Tim and Joyce formed a partnership with a builder to remodel a house for profit. The builder turned out to be dishonest, and they got stuck with house payments on two homes.

One day Joyce's father was expressing concern and asked, "How rough is it?"

"Oh, Dad," she said. "This is the greatest challenge to the strength of our marriage we have ever had to face. But, Dad, I wouldn't trade this time for anything. Tim and I have never felt more close to each other. We are reading the Bible together, and we are praying together like we have never done before. We are learning so much."

Here is the lesson: Never ask God to shorten the duration of your hard times. Rather, ask God to teach you every lesson He intends for you during your hard time, lest you have to travel that road again.

Read Psalm 66:5-12 in your Bible and describe how the suffering experienced by the Psalmist and his people became a blessing and a gift.

_____

_____

The Psalmist noted that God has tested His people and "refined" them. Suffering will make us bitter or better. The choice is ours. On the bar below, consider all the suffering you have experienced. Put an x to indicate where you are right now as a result of suffering.

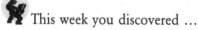

Better   Bitter

If you marked the bar toward the "Bitter" side, find a Christian friend or counselor with whom to share this feeling or attitude. Seek to be released from bitterness and freed by the power of Jesus Christ to grow and mature.

The Bottom Line
- Suffering is not just a test, it is also a blessing.
- Suffering in God's hands is a redemptive gift.
- Ask God to teach you every lesson He intends for you during your hard time, lest you have to travel that road again.
- Suffering will make us bitter of better.

This week you discovered ...
- the nature of suffering.
- where you are personally in understanding suffering.
- how to view suffering as a gift and a means for spiritual growth.

What does God want you to do in response to this week's study?

Recite Philippians 4:12-13 as a closing thought for the week.

FOUR CONSOLING TRUTHS ABOUT SUFFERING

Once during a message I gave near year-end I asked the men in the audience, "How many of you experienced great joy this past year? If so, please raise you hand." Every man in the room raised his hand.

Then I asked, "How many of you have experienced suffering this last year? If so, would you please raise your hand?" Again, every man in the room raised his hand.

Life simultaneously chugs along two tracks: the track of joy and the track of suffering. When my wife and I took our wedding vows, we conceded to the certainty of joy and suffering as we pledged our love "in sickness and in health, in plenty and in want, in joy and in sorrow, as long as we both shall live."

We all frequently find ourselves immersed in joy and sorrow at the same time. We lose a big sale after months of hard work, but come home to the news that our son or daughter made the basketball team. The boss brags about us in front of the whole company, but on the way home we must drop in on our aging parents who require daily supervision.

In the midst of these paradoxes, we can know certain truths about suffering. This week you will…

• Learn that suffering will always be a part of our lives on this earth.
• Begin to understand our calling and purpose in suffering.
• Experience the comfort God gives in the midst of suffering.

Some people believe that when a person becomes a Christian, all problems should cease. That is a naive view of reality. The truth is that, as Christians, we simply learn how to respond to and persevere through problems. And, we discover how to resist certain sins that cause suffering in our lives and the lives of others. Scripture asserts that we share in the sufferings of Jesus Christ, not that we avoid them.

★ DAY 1 ★ The Major Seasons of Suffering	★ DAY 2 ★ The Certainty of Suffering	★ DAY 3 ★ The Calling to Suffer
★ DAY 4 ★ The Purpose of Suffering	★ DAY 5 ★ The Comfort in Suffering	

Memorize and meditate on this verse this week.

"Just as the sufferings of Christ flow over into our lives, so also through Christ our comfort overflows" (2 Corinthians 1:5).

I pray that this week you will enjoy God's comfort in any suffering you experience and that you will understand more fully the calling and purpose of suffering in your life.

THE MAJOR SEASONS OF SUFFERING

Think for a moment of the great seasons of suffering in your life. I am not talking about opposition. Every day we face opposition–resistance–to leading a successful life. I'm speaking to those significant periods when circumstances collide and crash together to overwhelm you for a season.

◆

Every man experiences seasons of suffering throughout his life.

I am going to list my seasons of suffering for you (**in bold type**). After each statement will be a sentence for you to complete. Briefly describe such a season you may have experienced in your life. If you have not experienced that season, leave the description blank and go on to the next one.

1. **The period of *disillusionment* and *lack of meaning* that led me to drop out of high school.**
   A period of disillusionment and lack of meaning led me to...

   _____

   _____

2. **A prolonged time of *loneliness* and *emptiness* while in the army.**
   A time of loneliness and emptiness came when I...

   _____

   _____

3. The *despair* early in my marriage, which resulted in surrendering my life to Christ.
   A period of despair resulted in ...

   _____

   _____

4. Six months of depressed feelings from *unmet* business *expectations* and *financial pressure* early in my business career.
   My depressed feelings and unmet expectations in _____ led to...

   _____

   _____

5. Pain from migraine headaches, which deeply *discouraged* me.
   I became most discouraged when...

   _____

   _____

6. The tragic *death* of my younger brother.
   The death of _____ affected me most, and I...

   _____

   _____

7. Four years of *crisis, business troubles,* and *fear of failure* from the Tax Reform Act of 1986.
   Crises and fear of failure came when I...

   _____

   _____

No two- or three-day-long trifles, these seasons of suffering became my consuming focus for months on end—even though I tried to wear a mask and say, "Everything's just great."

Frankly, until we have suffered, not in some superficial way like not getting a new car we wanted, but as a Christian, filled with anguish over whether God cares about us or not, we will not have a full understanding of how personal the ministry of the Holy Spirit can be.

Until you have been up against the wall, totally backed into the corner, all your resources expended, no more ideas from your own ingenuity, no more wise counsel from friends, all favors owed have been called in; until you have been totally exhausted and without hope—not just for a moment—but for weeks and months or even years on end; not until then will trusting the Lord ever move entirely from abstract to personal.

You may know it in part, but until you come to the point that you feel you will die unless Jesus shows you some compassion, only then will you ever trust Him completely. Once you pass through this threshold of His grace, you will have incredible power to overcome anxiety. The tempter cannot terrorize you with any uncertainty which you have not already known; you have seen the hands of God reach down, responding to your faith.[1]

Has God used a time of suffering to move your relationship with Him from abstract to personal? Briefly describe the circumstances and how God worked in your life.

_____

_____

_____

_____

As we go through the suffering, trials, and tribulations of life, we discover certain relevant truths from God's Word that sustain us in each season of suffering. The next four days of study will uncover these truths.

31

What does God want you to do as a result of today's study?

_____

_____

The memory verse for the week gives us a foundation for understanding suffering. Repeat the verse aloud three or four times as a closing prayer and affirmation for this day.

"Just as the sufferings of Christ flow over into our lives, so also through Christ our comfort overflows" (2 Corinthians 1:5).

The Bottom Line
- Every man experiences seasons of suffering throughout his life.
- You may know it in part, but until you come to the point that you feel you will die unless Jesus shows you some compassion, only then will you ever trust Him completely.
- The tempter cannot terrorize you with any uncertainty which you have not already known; you have seen the hands of God reach down, responding to your faith.

---

[1]Patrick M. Morley, *The Man in the Mirror* (Nashville: Thomas Nelson, 1992), 243.

THE CERTAINTY OF SUFFERING

Faithful Christians suffer. About two and one half years ago, Daryll received a call that his wife had been in an automobile accident. Since that day, she has never had a full night's sleep. The synapses at the base of her skull were damaged, and the nerve endings make her sleep fitfully. It has put a real damper on their lives.

A Christian businessman faces bankruptcy. Another man who misses his daughter deals silently with an empty nest. Another man must cope with a teenager making all the wrong choices.

An attorney faces a dwindling practice against several competitors who advertise. A middle-aged man struggles to maintain his lifestyle on the reduced income of a new career. An older man struggles to adjust to the loss of his wife. A young man faces the daily depression of a pending divorce. Another man's marriage is not making it, and no one knows.

During the Passover meal, Jews symbolically dip parsley in salt water because "life is immersed in tears."

Joseph Parker said, "If you speak to broken hearts, you will always have a congregation. There is one in every pew."

We suffer in many ways. Here is a short list. Check all the different kinds of suffering you have experienced in recent months.
- ❑ Financial pain
- ❑ Relationship pain
- ❑ Emotional pain
- ❑ Physical pain
- ❑ Identity pain
- ❑ Pain from lack of purpose or direction
- ❑ Other pain: _____

◆

There is nothing you can do to avoid suffering in this life.

Suffering is certain. In this world you will suffer. Peter said, "Dear friends, do not be surprised at the painful trial you are suffering, as though something strange were happening to you" (1 Peter 4:12). Jesus said, "In this world you will have trouble" (John 16:33).

The Bible is not a book of fairy tales with each story having a happy ending. Rather, the Bible speaks of life realistically and reveals the God of all comfort who sees us through every difficulty in life.

From Genesis to Revelation, from creation to the present, the Bible describes a great cosmic struggle between the forces of good and the forces of evil culminating in human suffering. The prophets suffered. Jesus suffered. The disciples suffered. We suffer.

As John Guest put it, "We all have one choice to make: Each of us can suffer with Christ or without him."

We should expect to suffer, even for doing right. Suffering is certain. But some men believe that by careful planning they can avoid pain and suffering. They expect to circumvent pain by working hard and preparing for every circumstance.

I recently heard a minister speak who lives in a country that is being torn apart by a civil war. He told the story of a young man who worked with his family in the refugee area at the "front lines." They lived in one room of a facility flooded with refugees. They had a curfew each day and never knew when the next mortar shell or sniper fire might come near their building.

After several years, the mission agency decided he needed a break from the stress of living under these conditions. They sent him with his family to a neighboring country for a three month sabbatical of study and relaxation.

While they were there, his child broke his leg when he was struck by a car. His wife got sick and was hospitalized for several weeks. Another child fell out of a window and suffered minor injuries.

All the years they had been living in a war zone, they had never had any significant illness or injury. Now, during what was supposed to be a vacation, they suffered one setback after another.

The lesson is this, no matter where we are, we will suffer.

The minister closed his talk with an application for Christians in the West. Every time he comes to America, he is amazed at the time, money, and energy we spend to try to avoid inconvenience and suffering. Not only are all these efforts futile, but by spending our energy on them, we often miss the lessons that God has for us in our suffering.

There is nothing wrong with planning for the future or taking advantage of modern conveniences. But the expectation that these things will eliminate pain is unrealistic. Check the ways you have tried to eliminate future pain and inconvenience.

❏ Careful planning ❏ Technology
❏ Insurance ❏ Education
❏ Savings ❏ Developing coping skills and strategies
❏ Leisure pursuits ❏ Other: _____

Have these efforts ever worked? Think of a time when you suffered even though you were faithful to plan and prepare. Briefly describe that experience.

_____

_____

When we suffer, we have God's promise that He will be with us in our suffering. Read the following Psalm as a prayer of praise for how God walks with you through every difficulty in life.

I dwell in the shelter of the Most High and
   will rest in the shadow of the Almighty.
I will say of the Lord, "He is my refuge and my fortress,
   my God, in whom I trust."

Surely he will save me from the fowler's snare
   and from the deadly pestilence.
He will cover me with his feathers,
   and under his wings I will find refuge;
   his faithfulness will be my shield and rampart.
I will not fear the terror of night,
   nor the arrow that flies by day,
nor the pestilence that stalks in the darkness,
   nor the plague that destroys at midday.

A thousand may fall at my side,
    ten thousand at my right hand,
    but it will not come near me.
I will only observe with my eyes
    and see the punishment of the wicked.

If I make the Most High my dwelling—
    even the Lord, who is my refuge—
then no harm will befall me,
    no disaster will come near my tent.
For he will command his angels concerning me
    to guard me in all my ways;
they will lift me up in their hands,
    so that I will not strike my foot against a stone.
—Psalm 91 (personalized)

 What does God want you to do as a result of today's study?

_____

_____

The Bottom Line
- Faithful Christians suffer.
- There is nothing you can do to avoid suffering in this life.
- The Bible speaks of life realistically and reveals the God of all comfort who sees us through every difficulty in life.
- When we suffer, we have God's promise that He will be with us in our suffering.

THE CALLING TO SUFFER

Chuck Swindoll said, "For God to do an impossible work he must take an impossible man and crush him." The witty Jamie Buckingham was a bit more direct when he said with tongue in cheek, "He whom God loveth, he beateth the hell out of."

◆

**Today's Christian culture calls us to comfort,
the Bible calls us to suffer.**

Look over the following verses on suffering. Each one goes against the call to comfort that is evident today. Describe each verse in your own words, then circle a word or phrase that tells us what each verse says we can expect.

"It has been granted to you on behalf of Christ not only to believe on him, but also to suffer for him" (Philippians 1:29).

_____

_____

"To this you were called, because Christ suffered for you, leaving you an example, that you should follow in his steps" (1 Peter 2:21).

_____

_____

"Do not be surprised, my brothers, if the world hates you" (1 John 3:13).

_____

_____

" 'If the world hates you, keep in mind that it hated me [Jesus] first' " (John 15:18).

_____

_____

"In fact, everyone who wants to live a godly life in Christ Jesus will be persecuted" (2 Timothy 3:12).

In our contemporary world, suffering presents us with two choices. First, we can join in the crusade to shape the world into a utopia by seeking to eliminate all sources of potential pain. Or, second, we can accept that the "world in its present form is passing away" (1 Corinthians 7:31) and enter into the Bible's call to suffer.

Read each of the following passages in your Bible. What should be our attitude toward suffering based upon these verses? Have you ever considered suffering as a Christian calling? How do these verses affect your thinking?

• John 16:33 _____

• 1 Peter 4:12-14 _____

• James 1:2 _____

• Acts 14:22 _____

How willing and available to God are you to suffer for the sake of Jesus Christ? On the bars below, mark an x to indicate where you are.

I have suffered greatly for the Lord.	I have suffered very little for the Lord.

I am willing to suffer for Christ.	I am unwilling to suffer for Christ.

I am working to eliminate all suffering from my life.	I accept suffering I cannot change.

The call to suffer is at its simplest the call to follow Jesus Christ. Because He suffered, we too will suffer. Are you willing to accept the call? In closing today, write a prayer thanking Jesus Christ for suffering on your behalf. Express your willingness to accept God's call to suffer.

_____

_____

_____

_____

The Bottom Line
- Today's Christian culture calls us to comfort, the Bible calls us to suffer.
- The call to suffer is at its simplest the call to follow Jesus Christ.

THE PURPOSE OF SUFFERING

The Scriptures we have studied in the Season of Suffering indicate a *purpose* to suffering. Jesus suffered to redeem us from sin and death. We suffer with Christ to accomplish His eternal, spiritual purposes. People can handle almost any amount of evil and suffering if they believe it is for a purpose. Remove purpose, and suffering is intolerable.

When you suffer for Christ's sake, what purpose does it serve? From the biblical reasons listed below, check those that you have seen in your own life as a result of suffering.

❑ That we may be delivered from bondage and become children of God (Romans 8:20-21).

❑ That we will rely upon God, not ourselves (2 Corinthians 1:9).

❑ That we may be more sensitive to others, that we can comfort them with the comfort we ourselves have received (2 Corinthians 1:4; Luke 22:31-32).

❑ That through our sufferings, the saving grace of God will reach more people (2 Corinthians 4:15).

❑ That Christ may receive praise (1 Peter 1:6-7).

❑ That evil may be punished (Deuteronomy 9:4-5).

❑ That we may draw closer to God (2 Corinthians 1:4).

❑ That we will be corrected by discipline (Hebrews 12:5-11).

❑ That our character may be developed (Romans 5:3-5).

◆

There is no such thing as meaningless suffering.

That people suffer for no *apparent* reason does not mean there is no reason. Read the following verse and write it in your own words.

"We know that in all things God works for the good of those who love him, who have been called according to his purpose" (Romans 8:28).

_____

_____

Whatever befalls the believer, it works for his good (whether in this life or eternally we cannot be certain). Proverbs 12:21 puts it this way:
"No harm befalls the righteous,
    but the wicked have their fill of trouble."
The word for *harm* means "to come to naught or nothingness."[1] Nothing that happens to the righteous will "come to naught"—suffering is not meaningless.

As one man experiencing arrhythmia said, "My crisis was good—it brought me back to reality." It was not meaningless.

God puts things in front of us that are bigger than we are so we must depend upon Him.

Describe something God put in front of you that was difficult at the time but helped you learn to depend more on Him.

_____

_____

On a Sunday morning in a small Alabama town, a tornado ripped through a Methodist church during the worship service. In the disaster, the pastor's four-year-old child died. In a news conference, this pastor expressed a poignant truth: "We don't need faith for the things we understand. We need faith for the things we don't understand."

How does faith help in suffering? The Bible is our final court of appeal on matters of feeling and experience. We do not interpret our Bible by our experience; we interpret our experience by our Bible. In the end, you and I must live by faith. "We live by faith, not by sight" (2 Corinthians 5:7).

Put an x on the bar to indicate how you normally interpret suffering in your life.

I focus on my feelings, opinions, and experience.

I focus on the promises of God in Scripture.

41

Why should we base our understanding of suffering on the Bible rather than on our own experience? God's truth is not changed or altered by our experiences, reason, common sense, or opinions. The Bible doesn't always give us a precise answer to a particular situation. At that point we decide by faith to accept the mystery in the nature of God. The one question we cannot answer is, "Why is there suffering at all?" We simply don't know. "The secret things belong to the Lord our God" (Deuteronomy 29:29). But this we do know: God is good.

Though we cannot know why there is suffering at all, we do know from Romans 8:28 that God uses suffering for good. God is always working. If God calls a man to suffer, it is because that is how that man will grow. Pain is for growth. Pain is God's grace for growth.

 What does God want you to do as a result of today's study?

_____

_____

The Bottom Line
- People can handle almost any amount of evil and suffering if they believe it is for a purpose.
- There is no such thing as meaningless suffering.
- That people suffer for no *apparent* reason does not mean there is no reason.
- God puts things in front of us that are bigger than we are so we must depend upon Him.
- We do not interpret our Bible by our experience; we interpret our experience by our Bible.

---

[1] *Strong's Exhaustive Concordance of the Bible.*

THE COMFORT
IN SUFFERING

In the midst of suffering, God comforts us so that later we may also be a comfort to others. Some years ago I had finished speaking at an evangelistic prayer breakfast in Vero Beach, Florida. As I drove back to Orlando, I passed very near the site of the last property problem that could put me under.

I eased off the interstate and drove to the buildings. Workmen were building out a tenant space, but it was too little too late. I circled the buildings, drove slowly around to the back, parked my car, and got out.

The emotional tension this deal had produced was wrapped around my chest like tight steel bands. After glancing both ways to make sure no one was watching, I lay prostrate on the grass and prayed to God for deliverance and mercy.

Near the beginning of this fresh-in-my-memory season of suffering, I had discovered a wonderful promise from God: "Call upon me in the day of trouble; I will deliver you, and you will honor me" (Psalm 50:15). This promise is simple. If we call upon the Lord in our day of trouble, He will deliver us. But notice the promise also includes an obligation. The delivered man is instructed to honor the Lord.

Have you ever faced so severe a crisis or time of suffering that you desperately cried out to God having no other place to turn? If so, briefly describe your situation and the feelings you experienced.

_____

_____

When I first read Psalm 50:15, I made a pledge to God that if He would deliver me from my suffering, I would praise, honor, and glorify His name for His mercies, which is why I'm telling you this story.

Eventually, we were able to settle the business problem, and God did deliver me. And I followed the psalmist's instructions,

"Give thanks to the Lord, call on his name; make known among the nations what he has done" (Psalm 105:1).

Let me pose a tough question: What if God doesn't deliver you in the short term? What if suffering lasts for months and even years? Will you still continue to honor and praise Him? Or, will you be tempted to turn your back on God and possibly even curse Him?

Scripture tells us that Job faced almost every imaginable kind of suffering and still refused to curse God. He lost his children and their families, his wealth, his position in society, his health, and the respect of his wife and friends.

What is your attitude toward suffering? Check the sufferings that would be most difficult for you to endure and still honor God.

- ❑ Terminal disease attacking me
- ❑ Terminal disease attacking a loved one
- ❑ Tragic or violent death of a friend
- ❑ Deaths of innocent people
- ❑ Death of my wife
- ❑ Loss of my job
- ❑ Death of my child
- ❑ Loss of possessions

Although I pray that I never again go through a season of suffering like I went through, I truly thank God for suffering. Through my suffering, God reshaped my character and kept me from running headlong into certain disaster.

◆

Because there is purpose *to* suffering, there is comfort *in* suffering.

God knows what He is doing. God is completely dependable and trustworthy. We can count on Him. God will always do what is right. Through our suffering, God corrects our faulty thinking, spares us from greater evils, and brings about greater goods. God leads us to repent of our sins and produces in us the character of His Son, Jesus.

Suffering produces within us the ability to comfort others with the comfort we have experienced from God. Paul writes about it this way, "Praise be to the God and Father of our Lord Jesus Christ, the Father of compassion and the God of all comfort, who comforts us in all our troubles, so that we can comfort those in any trouble with the comfort we ourselves have received from God" (2 Corinthians 1:3-4).

Here are some ways we can comfort others. Check the ones you use most often.
- ❑ Listening
- ❑ Praying
- ❑ Just being there
- ❑ Sharing how God has comforted you
- ❑ Meeting physical or emotional needs
- ❑ Taking them to someone or someplace that can provide help
- ❑ Other: _____

Look over the list. Which display of grace and comfort means the most to you when you are suffering? Circle that one.

Think of how you have grown and matured through the tests, trials, afflictions, and sufferings in your life. The Bible indicates that we cannot become all God wants us to be without suffering. We need the grace of affliction. Yes, trials and tribulations are painful at the time, and we should never seek them out. Yet, when they come, they come as the sweet fragrance of God's grace to help us grow, mature, and stay on the right path. King David understood that affliction is actually a blessing.

Underline the phrases in the following selected passages that mean the most to you.
> It was good for me to be afflicted
> so that I might learn your decrees (Psalm 119:71).

> Before I was afflicted I went astray,
> But now I obey your word (Psalm 119:67).

> I know, O Lord, that your laws are righteous,
> and in faithfulness you have afflicted me (Psalm 119:75).

The Bible encourages you to "Cast all your anxiety on him because he cares for you" (1 Peter 5:7).

Charles' wife died after a lengthy battle with cancer. For many months he grieved deeply over the passing of his best friend. Indeed, she was an encouragement and source of increased faith to all who knew her. One day while riding in his car, Charles starting yelling at God in anguish. When he completely vented himself, the only thing left to do was to yell to God, "Now what?"

"Now what" for you? Where are you today? Perhaps you have made peace with suffering. Or maybe you are struggling to accept suffering as part of life. Perhaps you can't see any purpose to it. Possibly you long for joy to return. You may need to be comforted. Comfort is available. Come to Jesus. Throw yourself upon His mercy and goodness. Be patient and wait for Him to act. God will rescue you in due season.

The Bottom Line
- Because there is purpose *to* suffering, there is comfort *in* suffering.
- Through our suffering, God corrects our faulty thinking, spares us from greater evils, and brings about greater goods.
- Suffering produces within us the ability to comfort others with the comfort that we ourselves have experienced from God.

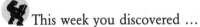 This week you discovered ...
- that suffering will always be a part of life.
- how we each have a calling and purpose in suffering.
- the comfort God gives in the midst of suffering.

What does God want you to do in response to this week's study?

_____

_____

Recite 2 Corinthians 1:5 as a closing thought for the week.

REFLECTING ON THIS SEASON

1. The most important truth I learned for my spiritual life:

_____

_____

2. The Scripture passage that spoke to me with the most meaning (write the scripture or your paraphrase of it):

_____

_____

_____

3. One thing I need to confess to the Lord and ask forgiveness for:

_____

4. One thing I need to praise the Lord for:

_____

5. One important change the Lord and I need to make in my life:

_____

6. The next step I need to take in obedience:

_____

FOUR ATTITUDES OF SUCCESSFUL MEN
(PART 1)

A ruddy young man bent down, reached into a trickling seasonal stream, selected five stones polished smooth by time, faced off against a nine-foot-tall giant who talked too much, hurled a single stone that sank deep into his forehead, cut off his head, and saved his people from annihilation. It was quite a day.

The people cheered their new hero, David. As a reward for his bravery, he rose to a high rank in the king's army, pleasing everyone. The Bible says, "In everything he did he had great success, because the Lord was with him" (1 Samuel 18:14). It was a season of success. This was David's beginning.

No man who ever lived has been more successful than David. The Bible records that "he died at a good old age, having enjoyed long life, wealth and honor" (1 Chronicles 29:28). That was his end.

In the coming three weeks, we will explore the Season of Success. We will consider four attitudes of successful men and how those attitudes are expressed in daily life.

As you study, be willing to challenge your notions of success and compare them to the Bible's truths. As you study, keep in mind the standard set for us in the life of King David: " 'I [God] have found David son of Jesse a man after my own heart; he will do everything I [God] want him to do' " (Acts 13:22).

During this first week in the Season of Success, we will ...
• Look at two attitudes of a successful man.
• Understand what it means to take risks for God, not our own selfish motives.
• Focus on how to conquer fear while standing firm in Jesus Christ.

★ DAY 1 ★
The
"Character of
David"
Test

★ DAY 2 ★
Attitude #1:
Take Some
Risks

★ DAY 3 ★
Conquering
Fear

★ DAY 4 ★
Attitude #2:
Depend on
God

★ DAY 5 ★
Trust in God
or Man?

Memorize and meditate on this memory verse:

The Lord will make you the head, not the tail. If you pay attention to the commands of the Lord your God that I give you this day and carefully follow them, you will always be at the top, never at the bottom (Deuteronomy 28:13).

THE "CHARACTER OF DAVID" TEST

What kind of man was David? God declared, "I have found David son of Jesse a man after my own heart; he will do everything I want him to do" (Acts 13:22). His heart was fully devoted to the Lord (see 1 Kings 11:4). God said David "kept my commands and followed me with all his heart, doing only what was right in my eyes" (1 Kings 14:8).

No man in the Bible ever received more approval from God than David. No man represents a better model for how we should live our lives. What more could you or I ever hope for than to be called a man after God's own heart?

◆

The key to our success is to be "a man after God's own heart."

God had a purpose for David's life. David "served God's purpose in his own generation" (Acts 13:36). God has a purpose for your life too.

David knew his success was not for himself only, but also for the sake of others. The Bible says, "David knew that the Lord had established him as king over Israel and had exalted his kingdom for the sake of his people Israel" (2 Samuel 5:12). Whatever success you and I enjoy, part of the reason God gives success is for the benefit of others.

David learned the secrets of success. He became a man favored by God. Are you such a man? Are you, like David, a man after God's own heart?

 Mark an x on each bar to indicate your answer to each question. Are you a man after God's own heart?

Always   Sometimes   Never

Will you do everything the Lord wants you to do?

Always   Sometimes   Never

Are you serving God's purpose in your generation?

Always   Sometimes   Never

Notice it's not perfection that God seeks but a willing, compliant heart. Is it your desire to be more devoted to trusting, loving, and obeying God? Are the marks on your bars from the middle to the left, from sometimes to always?

When you fail God, are you prompt to repent and willing to receive His guidance? David didn't *always* obey God. But his heart desired to obey God and repent when he failed. That's what it means to be a man after God's own heart.

The following passages reveal some other characteristics and attitudes that make people successful in God's eyes. Read them carefully, and then write a word or brief phrase to identify the heart attitude revealed.

Passages	Heart Attitudes
Love the Lord your God with all your heart and with all your soul and with all your strength (Deuteronomy 6:5).	_____ _____ _____
But I trust in your unfailing love; my heart rejoices in your salvation (Psalm 13:5).	_____ _____ _____
Create in me a pure heart, O God, and renew a steadfast spirit within me (Psalm 51:10).	_____ _____ _____
The sacrifices of God are a broken spirit; a broken and contrite heart, O God, you will not despise (Psalm 51:17).	_____ _____ _____

Teach me your way, O Lord,   _____
    and I will walk in your truth;   _____
give me an undivided heart,   _____
    that I may fear your name   _____
(Psalm 86:11).   _____

I have hidden your word in my heart   _____
    that I might not sin against you   _____
(Psalm 119:11).   _____

Where your treasure is, there your   _____
heart will be also (Matthew 6:21).   _____

Now that you have purified yourselves   _____
by obeying the truth so that you have   _____
sincere love for your brothers, love one   _____
another deeply, from the heart   _____
(1 Peter 1:22).   _____

Now look back over these heart attitudes. Circle those attitudes you have in some measure in your life. Check those attitudes you would like to work on.

David stands at the head of a long line of Bible heroes in the Old Testament after whom we can pattern our lives. God gave Nehemiah the vision to rebuild the city of his fathers. God anointed Daniel to preserve the kingdom of God while his nation was exiled to Babylon. God used Asa to reform Israel from its wicked ways. God sent Joseph to Egypt ahead of his family to save their lives. God called Noah to build an ark to preserve the human race. God raised up Moses to lead his people out of slavery.

If David and this gallery of heroes could speak to us from the grave, what advice would they give us about how to lead a successful life? What would they lay down as the attitudes of success? We will explore four attitudes this week and next.

Review today's lesson. What one Scripture was most meaningful to you today? Write it below.

_____

_____

Below is the memory verse for the week substituting the word *me* or *I* for the word *you*. Say the verse as a closing prayer.

The Lord will make [me] the head, not the tail. If [I] pay attention to the commands of the Lord [my] God ... this day and carefully follow them, [I] will always be at the top, never at the bottom (Deuteronomy 28:13).

The Bottom Line
- The key to our success is to be "a man after God's own heart."
- God has a purpose for your life.
- Whatever success you and I enjoy, part of the reason God gives success is for the benefit of others.

ATTITUDE #1: TAKE SOME RISKS

David and our gallery of biblical heroes would begin by advising, "Have the courage to take risks others are not willing to take." No one else would go out to fight Goliath, but David risked almost certain death and went. When everyone else's courage melted, David did not lose heart. So that you don't think he was some naive, inexperienced teenage boy, remember that this boy had a track record. He had killed both lion and bear with his bare hands. It was not an uncalculated risk.

◆

A successful man will take risks for God.

Like David, we should take more risks, but not without some calculation and preparation. Success is that point at which preparation meets opportunity. For example, it would be foolish to risk your life savings on a small business if you have no business experience at all. On the other hand, if God calls you to start your own business after serving as an administrator to another businessman for 15 years, perhaps you should take a calculated, considered risk.

Let's explore what mix of godly qualities inspire risking all for the Lord. The word that God has for us in Joshua 1 is *courage*. Courage means "to be strong, stand firm and secure." God says to Joshua, "Be strong and very courageous. Be careful to obey all the law my servant Moses gave you; do not turn from it to the right or to the left, that you may be successful wherever you go" (Joshua 1:7).

Taking risk involves standing firm on God's truth and strength. David knew his strength was from the Lord.

> The Lord is my light and my salvation—
> whom shall I fear?
> The Lord is the stronghold of my life—
> of whom shall I be afraid? ...
> Wait for the Lord;
> be strong and take heart
> and wait for the Lord (Psalm 27:1,14).

What qualities do you see in David as he faced Goliath? Check every courageous quality you see in him.

- ❏ Hopefulness
- ❏ Boldness
- ❏ Right timing
- ❏ Experience and perseverance
- ❏ Faith in God

If you checked all of the above, you are correct. In fact, all these qualities need to be present if we are to risk great things with God. If God is in it, we can risk anything with the confidence that He will see us through.

Think of a risk for God you could take right now. Understanding that faith in God is the foundation for taking any risk, what is the next quality from the above list that you would like to develop?

_____

Let's match each of these courageous qualities with an example or teaching from God's Word. Below are several passages of Scriptures. Write one of the qualities from the following list in the blank before each passage. The quality should identify the truth of the passage.

Hopefulness   Right timing   Faith in God
Boldness   Experience and perseverance

_____ Now faith is being sure of what we hope for and certain of what we do not see. This is what the ancients were commended for. By faith we understand that the universe was formed at God's command, so that what is seen was not made out of what was visible. ... Without faith it is impossible to please God, because anyone who comes to him must believe that he exists and that he rewards those who earnestly seek him (Hebrews 11:1-3,6).

_____ Not only so, but we also rejoice in our sufferings, because we know that suffering produces perseverance; perseverance, character; and character, hope. And hope does not disappoint us, because God has poured out his love into our hearts by the Holy Spirit, whom he has given us (Romans 5:3-5).

55

_____ I say to myself, "The Lord is my portion; therefore I will wait for him." The Lord is good to those whose hope is in him, to the one who seeks him (Lamentations 3:24-25).

_____ God did not give us a spirit of timidity, but a spirit of power, of love and of self-discipline (2 Timothy 1:7).

_____ Wait for the Lord; be strong and take heart and wait for the Lord (Psalm 27:14).

Each of these qualities of biblical courage and strength are needed to take divinely inspired risks. Many people never attempt anything significant because they might fail. Not Abraham, Joshua, Noah, Gideon, Daniel, or Paul. They heard God's calling on their lives and took calculated risks because they believed God was able to complete what He put in their hearts to do.

Review today's lesson. What one Scripture was most meaningful to you today? Write it below.

_____

_____

_____

What does God want you to do as a result of today's lesson?

_____

_____

_____

Offer a prayer celebrating that God can give you the courage to take risks for Him. Claim this verse as part of your prayer: "Being confident of this, that he who began a good work in you will carry it on to completion until the day of Christ Jesus" (Philippians 1:6).

The Bottom Line
- A successful man will take risks for God.
- We should take more risks, but not without some alculation and preparation.
- Many people never attempt anything significant because they might fail.

(Answers: Hebrews 11:1-3,6–Faith in God; Romans 5:3-5–Experience and Perseverance; Lamentations 3:24-25–Hopefulness; 2 Timothy 1:7–Boldness; Psalm 27:14–Right timing)

CONQUERING FEAR

Hudson Taylor said, "Many Christians estimate difficulties in light of their own resources, and thus attempt little and often fail in the little they do attempt. All God's giants have been weak men who did great things for God because they reckoned on His power and presence being with them."

◆

Courage is not the absence of fear but a willingness to trust God in the presence of fear.

Right now I'm investigating a drive-time radio show for men. Frankly, my strongest impulse is not to do it. Why? Fear. What if it fails? What if people don't like me? What if I can't fund it? What if I'm criticized? Or worse still, ridiculed?

Do you have great fears in your life that paralyze you? Here are some common things which cause men to have fears. Check those you experience regularly.

❑ losing my job   ❑ marriage dissolving
❑ rebellious child   ❑ not being good enough for God
❑ being rejected   ❑ being ridiculed
❑ being criticized   ❑ going to hell
❑ not providing financially   ❑ other: _____

In yesterday's activities we looked at Joshua 1:7 where God told Joshua to be strong and courageous. It is interesting that He repeated the command two verses later. "Be strong and very courageous," He said. "Do not be terrified; do not be discouraged, for the Lord your God will be with you wherever you go" (Joshua 1:9). God's presence in our lives is the wellspring that brings forth courage. If you have never trusted Christ, read John 3:16 below.

"For God so loved the world that he gave his one and only Son, that whoever believes in him shall not perish but have eternal life."

Pray this prayer from your heart.

Lord Jesus, I surrender my whole self to You. I repent of my sins. I confess You to be the Son of God, the Christ, and I receive You as my Lord and Savior. Thank You for shedding Your blood on the cross for my sins. I receive the gift of Your Holy Spirit and will live for You. Amen.

If you prayed this prayer, share your decision to follow Christ with another Christian. Your experience in this study will take on new meaning because of your decision.

Fifty people over the age of 95 were asked on an open-ended basis, "If you could live your life over again, what would you do differently?" As you can imagine, the answers covered a wide range. However, one answer that kept showing up over and over was this: "If I had it to do over again, I would risk more."[1] Are you afraid to stick your neck out on something God is leading you to do?

Jesus once told a story that contrasted two risk takers with someone who let fear inhibit his ability to "stick his neck out." That parable, recorded in Matthew 25:14-30, begins with a man who was leaving on a journey. He called his three servants together and entrusted each of them with a sum of money based on their abilities. To the first he gave five talents, to the second he gave two talents, and to the third he gave one talent.

The first two went out immediately and invested the funds their master had entrusted to them, and they each doubled their money. Needless to say, the master was pleased when he returned.

The last servant, though, came with bad news. "Master," he said, "I knew that you are a hard man, ... So I was afraid and went out and hid your talent in the ground." He was able to bring back the original amount, but he had no gains to report.

The master replied, "You wicked, lazy servant!" And he took away that servant's talent and gave it to the man who started out with 5 and made it into 10.

Which servant do you honestly identify with? The servant with...
❑ Five talents   ❑ Two talents   ❑ One talent

Based on this parable, what is God's attitude toward taking risks?

_____

In closing today, be honest with yourself. Where have you been less than courageous in your life?

_____

Over and over again in Scripture, God's messengers tell those to whom they are sent, "Fear not." How can you change your thinking so that fear will no longer inhibit your ability to take divinely-inspired risks?

_____

_____

Who can you talk to for advise and counsel? _____

The Bottom Line
- All God's giants have been weak men who did great things for God because they reckoned on His power and presence being with them.
- Courage is not the absence of fear but a willingness to trust God in the presence of fear.
- God's presence in our lives is the wellspring that brings forth courage.

---

[1]Tony Campolo, *Who Switched the Price Tags?* (Dallas: Word, 1986), 28-29.

ATTITUDE #2:
DEPEND ON GOD

Let's check back with David and our biblical heroes. They would tell us, "Do everything you do in the name of the Lord." David was scrupulous to follow the Lord's leading. The few times he acted in the flesh he suffered deeply. Many people died when he took a forbidden census; and when he committed adultery with Bathsheba, the baby born to them died. He was human. So are we. But David learned to repent and give God glory in all things. God gave David victory and success in return.

◆

So closely identify everything you do with God that before men can prevail against you, they must first prevail against God.

One of our greatest temptations is to turn our strengths into feeble gods. Which of the following do you find yourself depending on from time to time instead of the Lord? Check all that apply.
- ❏ a good plan   ❏ experience
- ❏ natural ability   ❏ resources
- ❏ strength of will and character ❏ other people
- ❏ integrity   ❏ other:_____

Think of the last thing you risked for God. How much did you truly depend on God? Check one answer.
❏ I relied on myself. ❏ I "tipped my hat" to God. ❏ I relied on God.

One of Judah's kings that trusted God was Asa. He was a relentless reformer. He cleaned up the nation and made laws that required people to seek the Lord and obey His commandments. He created an economic boom and prospered, but what did he get for his labors? An army of one million troops marched against him.

Asa responded, "Lord, there is no one like you to help the powerless against the mighty. Help us, O Lord our God, for we rely on you, and in your name we have come against this vast army. O Lord, you are our God; do not let man prevail against you" (2 Chronicles 14:11).

I picture Asa running around telling everyone, "Hey! Don't worry about these guys. We rely on God! There's no one like God. We'll go out against this army in the name of the Lord! They can't whip us until they finish whipping God!"

Whose reputation was at stake in this risk?
❏ Asa's ❏ the Army's ❏ God's

If you answered God's, you are correct. If God is in a plan, then His reputation is at stake, not ours, to make the plan a success. Today, too many men think they are saved by faith, but somehow the rest is up to them. They have *saving* faith, but not *living* faith. God wants us to live all of our lives with His name on our lips.

Dependence on God does not imply a lack of strength. In fact, men who understand and admit their weaknesses have discovered real strength. Paul understood that God's strength could be best revealed in our weakness.

Read 2 Corinthians 12:9-10 below. Summarize it in your own words.

"[Jesus] said to me, 'My grace is sufficient for you, for my power is made perfect in weakness.' Therefore I will boast all the more gladly about my weaknesses, so that Christ's power may rest on me. That is why, for Christ's sake, I delight in weaknesses, in insults, in hardships, in persecutions, in difficulties. For when I am weak, then I am strong."

_____

_____

Dependence on God is the only way to achieve godly success. When we succeed in our own strength, our egos swell up in pride and the achievement only lasts for a brief time. When God accomplishes His plans through us, the results are lasting and eternal. God receives the glory, not us.

Dependence on God involves a surrender of pride and egotism, a replacing of pride with humility. Consider the following areas of your life. Shade each bar to the degree that it is fully dependent upon God. Ten represents "fully dependent on God."

	Finances	Marriage	Parenting	Work	Future Plans
10					
9					
8					
7					
6					
5					
4					
3					
2					
1					

In closing, write a brief prayer surrendering those areas of your life where you would like Jesus to take full control.

_____

_____

The Bottom Line
- So, closely identify everything you do with God that before men can prevail against you, they must first prevail against God.
- Dependence on God is the only way to achieve godly success.
- When God accomplishes His plans through us, the results are lasting and eternal.

TRUST IN GOD OR MAN?

I was very active in the human potential movement in the early 1970s. Every book that expounded the merits of willing-your-way-to-success was in my library. "What the mind can conceive and believe it can achieve," went the reasoning.

It would have been difficult to be in the marketplace during the self-centered 70s and the alienated 80s and not be at least partially influenced to believe "you can have it all." We Christians don't have any special inoculation against the desire to be independent.

It's true. By the power of our might and the strength of our own hands, we *can* achieve many worldly successes. The problem is, however, that God doesn't want us to trust in ourselves but rather to trust in Him.

◆

True success is a by-product of complete dependence on Jesus Christ.

Read the following verses from the Book of Jeremiah. Underline phrases that describe the fate of the man who trusts in himself.

" 'Cursed is the one who trusts in man,
who depends on flesh for his strength
and whose heart turns away from the Lord.
He will be like a bush in the wastelands;
he will not see prosperity when it comes.
He will dwell in the parched places of the desert,
in a salt land where no one lives' " (Jeremiah 17:5-6).

The man who depends on his own strength or trusts in the value system of this world will be miserable. The kind of man God speaks of in this passage is not some wicked sort of evil fellow. Rather the Bible describes a valiant man—someone who is a winner by all external appearances. But inside he has turned his heart away from the Lord. Like a bush which bears no seed, he tumbles along producing no fruit, headed nowhere.

The independent man is never able to satisfy his thirst for significance and purpose. We all know men who live in opulence, yet their creased faces betray a life of independence lived in parched places.

How have you experienced the dryness that comes from trying to live independently from God? Briefly describe that experience.

_____

_____

Read the next two verses from chapter 17 of Jeremiah. Underline phrases that describe the fate of the man who trusts in God.
" 'But blessed is the man who trusts in the Lord,
    whose confidence is in him.
He will be like a tree planted by the water
    that sends out its roots by the stream.
It does not fear when heat comes;
    its leaves are always green.
It has no worries in a year of drought
    and never fails to bear fruit' " (Jeremiah 17:7-8).
When we look closely at this passage we read, "It does not fear when *heat* comes," and "It has no worries in a year of *drought.*" Is Jeremiah describing an oasis? Hardly. The Christian is not exempt from hard times.

The difference between the man who trusts in God and the man who trusts in himself is not in the circumstances, but in his response. The man who trusts God knows that hard times will come, but he does not fear them. He does not dread the future, because he believes God will take care of him.[1]

Have you trusted God during "heat" and "drought"? Check any of the following you've experienced while continuing to trust God.
❑ difficulties in marriage   ❑ health problems
❑ financial difficulties   ❑ rebellious children
❑ relationships at work   ❑ fears about the future
How would your response to these things have been different if you had trusted in yourself rather than God?

_____

We are not independent, self-sustaining beings; rather we depend on God for health, provision, circumstances, and the future. A man will only find true success as he lives in daily, step-by-step dependence on God.

Paul described depending on Christ as being crucified with Him. Read Galatians 2:20 below, and rewrite it as a prayer to move you to more total dependence on God.

> I have been crucified with Christ and I no longer live, but Christ lives in me. The life I live in the body, I live by faith in the Son of God, who loved me and gave himself for me.

The Bottom Line
- True success is a by-product of complete dependence on Jesus Christ.
- The independent man is never able to satisfy his thirst for significance and purpose.
- The man who trusts God knows that hard times will come, but he does not fear them.
- A man will only find true success as he lives in daily, step-by-step dependence on God.

---

[1]Patrick M. Morley, *The Man in the Mirror* (Nashville: Thomas Nelson, 1992), 227-228.

This week you discovered ...
- that a successful man will take risks for God.
- that dependence on God is the only way to achieve godly success.
- how to conquer fear while standing firm in Jesus Christ.

What does God want you to do in response to this week's study?

FOUR ATTITUDES OF SUCCESSFUL MEN
(PART 2)

In considering the life of David and other Old Testament heroes, we identified four attitudes of success. Last week we explored two of those attitudes.

Attitude #1: Take some risks

Attitude #2: Depend on God

This week we will uncover the next two and the implications that accompany them.

Attitude #3: Take responsibility

Attitude #4: Expect opposition

As we study these two attitudes for biblical success during the coming days, we will...

• Discover that we have a responsibility to serve God.

• Learn to expect to be involved with opposition and spiritual warfare.

The devil doesn't want us to succeed. Our success is a light in the darkness, a witness to the world of the power of Jesus Christ. So, the devil will oppose us. But we can overcome opposition because our faith is rooted in Jesus Christ. Success always comes with a price. It begins with courage and moves forward in complete dependence on God. While costly, godly success pays eternal dividends for the kingdom of God.

★ DAY 1 ★
Attitude #3:
Take
Responsibility

★ DAY 2 ★
Being
Responsible
for Obedience

★ DAY 3 ★
Attitude #4:
Expect
Opposition

★ DAY 4 ★
Sources of
Opposition

★ DAY 5 ★
Spiritual
Warfare

As you study this week, it is my prayer that God will open your mind and heart to hear His challenge to you. I pray you will not merely seek God's blessing on your plans but rather become a blessing to others as God works His plan through you.

Memorize and meditate on this verse throughout the week.

Do not let this Book of the Law depart from your mouth; meditate on it day and night, so that you may be careful to do everything written in it. Then you will be prosperous and successful (Joshua 1:8).

ATTITUDE #3: TAKE RESPONSIBILITY

Muhammad Ali was describing a religious experience to a reporter. The reporter said, "It must be a great comfort to know that God is with you there in the corner of the ring." Ali replied, "Yes, it is a great comfort, but make no mistake about it. When the bell rings, that guy on the other side of the ring comes over and hits *me!*"

David depended completely on God, but it wasn't God who hurled the stone or cut off Goliath's head—David did.

◆

You must take personal responsibility for the outcome of your life.

The license plate on a friend's car reads: UP 2 YOU. "I'm tired of Christians blaming others and using that as an excuse for not making a contribution," he says. "We must go on from here. You have to take personal responsibility for who you are and what you will become."

 Do you find yourself taking personal responsibility for what's happening in your life? Put an x on the bars to indicate where you identify yourself right now.

Take personal responsibility   Blame others

React defensively
to criticism   Learn from
criticism

Admit when I'm wrong   Make excuses

Take the first step in
reconciliation and forgiveness   Expect others to
take the first step

At first these two ideas—depend on God and take responsibility—look as if they contradict each other. On further examination, though, we see they are complementary. We could put it this way:
- Success is the result of God's blessing, not man's effort.
- Success does not depend on man's effort, but rarely comes without hard work.

What is your response to these statements? Mark an x on the bar below to indicate if you agree or disagree with these statements.

Agree strongly   Agree in part   Disagree strongly

Let's review some Old Testament Scriptures that talk about success and our responsibility in it. Look at the following statements and briefly write what they say about success and our responsibility.

Passage   **Biblical success**

The Lord commanded us to obey all   _____
these decrees and to fear the Lord our   _____
God, so that we might always prosper   _____
and be kept alive, as is the case today.   _____
And if we are careful to obey all this   _____
law before the Lord our God, as he has   _____
commanded us, that will be our   _____
righteousness (Deuteronomy 6:24-25).   _____

A generous man will prosper;   _____
    he who refreshes others will himself   _____
    be refreshed (Proverbs 11:25).   _____

"Be strong and very courageous. Be   _____
careful to obey all the law my servant   _____
Moses gave you; do not turn from it   _____
to the right or to the left, that you may   _____
be successful wherever you go"   _____
(Joshua 1:7-8).   _____

70

Work hard. You can't expect God to work if you don't work. Aggressively follow up whatever God reveals for you to do. Be thankful for whatever God decides to do.

The apostle Paul put it this way: "I worked harder than all of them—yet not I, but the grace of God that was with me" (1 Corinthians 15:10). Even though he worked very hard, Paul attributed his efforts to the grace of God at work within him. In essence, he was saying, "I worked hard, but I always knew it depended on God, not me."

Dwight L. Moody put it this way: "We pray like it is all up to God. We work like it is all up to us." This makes good theology.

Working hard will not guarantee success, but not working hard will guarantee failure. Unfortunately, success does not always come in direct proportion to the amount of effort we put forth, but failure usually comes in direct proportion to our laziness. God is not calling men to be successful; He is calling men to be faithful.

Are you being faithful to God? On the bar below, place an x to indicate where you are right now in your faithfulness to God's plan for your life.

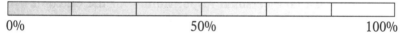

0%   50%   100%

If we are faithful, we will be successful in the way God wants us to be, and that should be enough. If it's not, we've got a problem. Christian men living in a world that has become a festering sore of violence, crime, drugs, poverty, racism, and despair can no longer afford to view success the way the world views success—through the narrow lens of "What's in it for me?"

To what extent have you been judging success based on your goals and ambitions apart from God? Mark an x on the bar to indicate your answer.

Self-centered   God-centered

What does God want you to do as a result of today's study?

_____

_____

In closing today, write a prayer asking God's Spirit to help you over-come any selfishness or laziness, and create a deep desire within you to take responsibility for your life.

_____

_____

The Bottom Line
- **You must take personal responsibility for the outcome of your life.**
- **Aggressively follow up whatever God reveals for you to do; be thankful for whatever God decides to do.**
- **Working hard will not guarantee success, but not working hard will guarantee failure.**
- **God is not calling men to be successful; He is calling men to be faithful.**

BEING RESPONSIBLE FOR OBEDIENCE

Taking responsibility for our lives will never happen if we rely only on our own wisdom and strength. We must discover God's purpose and plan for our lives. As Zechariah 4:6 reveals, " 'Not by might nor by power, but by my Spirit,' says the Lord Almighty."

The bottom line is that most of the time we won't have to wonder what God wants us to do. The Bible is full of His admonitions regarding our attitudes and behaviors.

◆

A successful man will take responsibility to obey God's Word.

For more extensive study, I recommend that you take a look at Matthew 5-7, where Jesus outlines the sweeping changes He wants to see in people's lives when they come into His kingdom. But for now, take a look at the following verses. On the lines at the right, briefly record the tasks or attitudes that should be present in the life of every successful man.

Jesus replied, " 'Love the Lord your God with all your heart and with all your soul and with all your mind.' This is the first and greatest commandment. And the second is like it: 'Love your neighbor as yourself' " (Matthew 22:37-39).

He has showed you, O man, what is good. And what does the Lord require of you? To act justly and to love mercy and to walk humbly with your God (Micah 6:8).

"Is not this the kind of fasting I [God] _____
have chosen: to loose the chains of _____
injustice and untie the cords of the _____
yoke, to set the oppressed free and _____
break every yoke? Is it not to share _____
your food with the hungry and to _____
provide the poor wanderer with shelter— _____
when you see the naked, to clothe him, _____
and not to turn away from your own _____
flesh and blood?" (Isaiah 58:6-7). _____

If we need God's wisdom to know how to apply biblical guidelines specifically to our lives, all we need to do is ask. Scripture tells us, "If any of you lacks wisdom, he should ask God, who gives generously to all without finding fault, and it will be given to him" (James 1:5).

True success is not determined by our abilities, but by our humble availability to be used by God. We must take responsibility to become servants of Christ.

In the following passage, the prophet Isaiah makes himself totally available to be used by God. Read the story and circle the part that speaks the most to you right now.

In the year that King Uzziah died, I saw the Lord seated on a throne, high and exalted, and the train of his robe filled the temple. Above him were seraphs, each with six wings: With two wings they covered their faces, with two they covered their feet, and with two they were flying. And they were calling to one another:

"Holy, holy, holy is the Lord Almighty;
   the whole earth is full of his glory."

At the sound of their voices the doorposts and thresholds shook and the temple was filled with smoke.

"Woe to me!" I cried. "I am ruined! For I am a man of unclean lips, and I live among a people of unclean lips, and my eyes have seen the King, the Lord Almighty."

Then one of the seraphs flew to me with a live coal in his hand, which he had taken with tongs from the altar. With it

he touched my mouth and said, "See, this has touched your lips; your guilt is taken away and your sin atoned for."
Then I heard the voice of the Lord saying, "Whom shall I send? And who will go for us?"
And I said, "Here am I. Send me!" (Isaiah 6:1-8).

Isaiah was a success in God's eyes because he was available. He acknowledged his inability and sinfulness. In his weakness, God was strong.

How available are you to God? ❑ always ❑ sometimes ❑ never

Ultimately, God will hold us all responsible for our own lives. He will hold us accountable for our actions and reactions, our beliefs and behaviors, our attitudes and thought patterns. Look up Matthew 25:31-46 in your Bible and reflect on it for a moment. Think about the way God holds people responsible for their lives in this parable. As you know by now, I believe strongly in the importance of accountability. Having someone to hold us accountable in this life will certainly help us stay on track in preparation for the accountability of eternity.

Within the realm of your close friends, whom can you rely on to hold you accountable? _____
If you haven't already done so, will you ask that person or those people to help you be responsible for your life? ❑ yes ❑ no
If yes, how will you go about it?

The Bottom Line
- A successful man will take responsibility to obey God's Word.
- If we need God's wisdom to know how to apply biblical guidelines specifically to our lives, all we need to do is ask.
- True success is not determined by our abilities, but by our humble availability to be used by God.

ATTITUDE #4:
EXPECT OPPOSITION

When Nehemiah heard that the captives who returned to Jerusalem from the Babylonian captivity had not been able to rebuild their city, even after 11 years, God put a vision in his heart to help them rebuild the city and the wall around it.

In two or three sentences, describe a significant task or calling that you believe God is asking you to do.

_____

_____

_____

As you consider this calling, where do you think you will find opposition? Check all that apply.

❏ Family   ❏ Spouse
❏ Coworkers   ❏ Self
❏ Friends   ❏ Satan
❏ Enemies   ❏ Other:_____

God provided Nehemiah with all the resources he needed to rebuild the city where he grew up. But when Nehemiah began to rebuild, he encountered stiff opposition. Opposition came from enemies who taunted them, rubble that discouraged them, famine that debilitated them, taxes that sapped them, and slavery that dehumanized them. They suffered through external threats, natural disasters, government interference, and economic hardships.

◆

The successful man expects opposition
even when he is doing God's will.

The problem with life is that there is opposition. A young man who had played especially well during basketball training camp did awful in his first game. The coach pulled him aside and asked, "What's going on?"

The young man said, "Coach, I would be doing great, but there are all these tall guys running around waving their hands in my face!"

In a fallen world we must expect opposition.

Below is a list adapted from 2 Corinthians 11:16-33 of many of the hardships Paul faced in spreading the gospel throughout the known world. Check any oppositions you have faced in obeying God's plan for your life.

❑ Worked harder and harder ❑ Was imprisoned
❑ Risked physical death ❑ Opposed by religious leaders
❑ Spent sleepless nights ❑ Fled persecution
❑ Faced natural disasters ❑ Criticized by hypocrites
❑ Went without food or water ❑ Risked much financially
❑ Went without essentials such as clothes or shelter
❑ In danger from government officials or agencies

As you look over the list, you may not have checked many items. If so, rejoice. You have not experienced the kind of opposition Paul faced. The question each of us should consider is, What would I be willing to endure for the Lord's sake?

When Paul was writing to tell the Corinthians he wanted to visit them, he said, "I will stay on at Ephesus until Pentecost, because a great door for effective work has opened to me, and there are many who oppose me" (1 Corinthians 16:8-9). Great opportunity is accompanied by great opposition. Paul produced fruit, but not without resistance.

When you face opposition for the Lord's sake, how do you respond? Circle the responses most common for you.

Anger	Hurt	Resentment	Joy
Withdrawal	Hope	Confidence	Determination
Increased faith	Doubt	Caution	Fear
Anxiety	Happiness	Patience	Impatience

There are times when the very person you expected to be supportive of you turns out to offer the most opposition to God's vision in your life. But if you expect opposition, you will be prepared for it when it happens. You can avoid the negative feelings that may arise, and you can learn to respond to resistance in a godly manner.

How can you respond to opposition? Here are four Scripture passages that address expecting opposition and responding to it. Underline words or phrases that express the ways we can respond to opposition.

> We had previously suffered and been insulted in Philippi, as you know, but with the help of our God we dared to tell you his gospel in spite of strong opposition (1 Thessalonians 2:2).

> "Endure hardship with us like a good soldier of Christ Jesus" (2 Timothy 2:3).

> Therefore, since we are surrounded by such a great cloud of witnesses, let us throw off everything that hinders and the sin that so easily entangles, and let us run with perseverance the race marked out for us. Let us fix our eyes on Jesus, the author and perfecter of our faith, who for the joy set before him endured the cross, scorning its shame, and sat down at the right hand of the throne of God. Consider him who endured such opposition from sinful men, so that you will not grow weary and lose heart (Hebrews 12:1-3).

> "Blessed are those who are persecuted because of righteousness,
>   for theirs is the kingdom of heaven.
> Blessed are you when people insult you, persecute you and falsely say all kinds of evil against you because of me. Rejoice and be glad, because great is your reward in heaven, for in the same way they persecuted the prophets who were before you" (Matthew 5:10-12).

Nehemiah handled his opposition this way: "Therefore I stationed some of the people behind the lowest points of the wall ... with their swords, spears and bows. ... From that day on, half of my men did the work, while the other half were equipped with spears, shields, bows and armor" (Nehemiah 4:13,16). Nehemiah depended on the Lord but also took responsibility for the call God put on his life. Because he expected opposition, Nehemiah was prepared and not overwhelmed.

Where are you getting opposition? Are you surprised? Are you prepared so you will not be overwhelmed? The next two days we will explore how to endure persecution and how to be prepared for spiritual warfare.

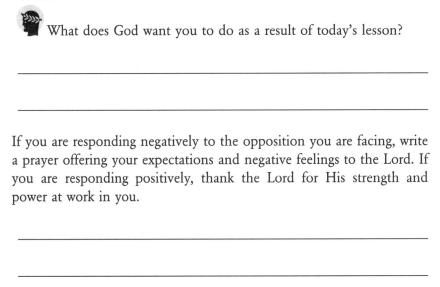 What does God want you to do as a result of today's lesson?

_____

_____

If you are responding negatively to the opposition you are facing, write a prayer offering your expectations and negative feelings to the Lord. If you are responding positively, thank the Lord for His strength and power at work in you.

_____

_____

The Bottom Line
- The successful man expects opposition even when he is doing God's will.
- Great opportunity is accompanied by great opposition.

SOURCES OF OPPOSITION

We have identified four essential attitudes for success.

Attitude #1: Take risks

Attitude #2: Depend on God

Attitude #3: Take responsibility

Attitude #4: Expect opposition

When we are truly living to please Jesus Christ, we can expect opposition from at least one of four sources.

◆

**Opposition comes from within, from the world,
from hypocrites, and from Satan.**

- **From within.** A war rages in every man between his spiritual and sinful natures.
- **From the world.** The world system opposes the gospel message and the growth of God's kingdom.
- **From religious hypocrites.** Religious people who don't understand God's ways and who live legalistic lives are critical and judgmental of God's people.
- **From Satan and the forces of evil.** The devil and his hosts seek to deceive, destroy, and distract from God's plan.

The first step in facing real opposition is to determine where the attack is coming from. Let's explore each source of opposition and what Scripture says we can expect. In knowing our enemy, we can effectively prepare for and resist attacks.

First, there is the attack **from within**: our sinful nature (flesh) attacks our spiritual nature. "So I say, live by the Spirit, and you will not gratify the desires of the sinful nature. For the sinful nature desires what is contrary to the Spirit, and the Spirit what is contrary to the sinful nature. They are in conflict with each other, so that you do not do what you want. But if you are led by the Spirit, you are not under law" (Galatians 5:16-18).

How do you prepare for attacks from within? Here is a list of suggestions. Check those you do most and circle those you can incorporate so to successfully resist attacks from within.

- ❑ Look at and listen to what is pure and godly
- ❑ Memorize Scripture
- ❑ Use my time to serve Christ
- ❑ Spend time in prayer and Bible study
- ❑ Refuse to accept glory that belongs to God
- ❑ Worship God regularly
- ❑ Keep my tongue from profanity, gossip, and hurting others
- ❑ Be in an accountability group with other Christian men
- ❑ Confess sin immediately
- ❑ Refuse to hate
- ❑ Refuse to hold on to hurts and bitterness

We also experience the attack **from the world**. The world system tempts us to do things selfishly for our own pleasure and self-serving motives. In the world system, we are enticed to gain glory for ourselves and to ask continually, "What's in it for me?"

The apostle John offers guidance on facing opposition from the world. Circle or underline what he identifies as coming from the world.

Do not love the world or anything in the world. If anyone loves the world, the love of the Father is not in him. For everything in the world—the cravings of sinful man, the lust of his eyes and the boasting of what he has and does—comes not from the Father but from the world" (1 John 2:15-16).

The world's system attacks Christianity at almost every point. God commands us to be servants. The world tempts us to be served. The world says *get* and *possess*; the Word says *give* and *surrender*. The world offers glory; biblical success understands that all glory belongs to God.

What is one attack you are currently experiencing from the world? Describe that attack and what you will do to resist.

_____

_____

Next there is the attack **from religious hypocrites**. Religious hypocrites attack God's purpose with tradition, legalism, and self-righteousness. You may be told you shouldn't proceed with God's plan for your life because it goes against traditions, practices, and established ways. Religious leaders can so carefully guard religious traditions that they fail to see God at work in the lives of others. Jesus warned the religious leaders of His day, "Woe to you, teachers of the law and Pharisees, you hypocrites! You shut the kingdom of heaven in men's faces. You yourselves do not enter, nor will you let those enter who are trying to" (Matthew 23:13).

Check any of the following religious attacks that you have experienced against God's vision for you.
- ❑ Legalism
- ❑ Self-righteous judgment
- ❑ Undue criticism
- ❑ Rejection
- ❑ Restrictive policies and procedures
- ❑ The attitude "We've never done it that way before"
- ❑ Pressure to conform to religious "culture"
- ❑ Discouragement and negativity
- ❑ Pressure to conform to man-made rules
- ❑ Other:_____

Finally, there is the attack **from Satan and the forces of evil**. Spiritual opposition will always be real when a Christian man follows God's plan for his life. Spiritual warfare will continue without ceasing as long as we live for Christ. To know the devices of Satan and the ways he attacks is important in living a successful Christian life. Tomorrow we will explore how to prepare for and engage in spiritual warfare.

If you are under attack from within, from religious hypocrites, or from the world, turn to God and seek His protection and power. God has made you a conqueror in Jesus Christ. You are already a victor and not a victim.

Review today's lesson carefully. What does God want you to do as a result of your study?

_____

_____

As a closing prayer, pray this verse out loud: "It is not by sword or spear that the Lord saves; for the battle is the Lord's, and he will give all of you [the enemy] into our hands" (1 Samuel 17:47).

The Bottom Line
- Opposition comes from within, from the world, from hypocrites, and from Satan.
- A war rages in every man between his spiritual and sinful natures.
- The world system opposes the gospel message and the growth of God's kingdom.
- Religious people who don't understand God's ways and who live legalistic lives are critical and judgmental of God's people.
- The devil and his hosts seek to deceive, destroy, and distract from God's plan.

SPIRITUAL WARFARE

As you try to live out God's calling on your life, you can be sure storms will come. Read the story of the wise man who built his house on a rock.

"Therefore everyone who hears these words of mine and puts them into practice is like a wise man who built his house on the rock. The rain came down, the streams rose, and the winds blew and beat against that house; yet it did not fall, because it had its foundation on the rock" (Matthew 7:24-25).

It's not a matter of *if* a storm will come, only a matter of *when* it will come. It's important as Christian men that we understand how Satan attacks and what kind of opposition we can expect.

◆

**The attacks of Satan are a powerful storm that
every Christian man must face.**

Below is a true/false test about Satan. See how well you know your enemy. Write *true* or *false* in each blank.

_____ 1. Satan doesn't know your future but you know that God will someday crush him (Romans 16:20).

_____ 2. Satan is the father of lies but you have been set free by God's truth (John 8:44).

_____ 3. Satan has no power over you; he is under your heel (Romans 16:20).

_____ 4. You can resist Satan by humbling yourself and following Christ (James 4:7).

All of these statements are true. Satan does not have the attributes of God. He is not all-knowing, all-powerful, or all-present—only God is. Therefore, don't give a foothold to Satan.

How have you underestimated the influence of Satan on your life?

_____

_____

How have you given Satan too much credit and overemphasized his power?

_____

_____

The passages below describe the attacks of Satan and his forces of evil. Read each Scripture and underline the tactic Satan uses.

Satan … masquerades as an angel of light (2 Corinthians 11:14).

The coming of the lawless one will be in accordance with the work of Satan displayed in all kinds of counterfeit miracles, signs and wonders (2 Thessalonians 2:9).

Be self-controlled and alert. Your enemy the devil prowls around like a roaring lion looking for someone to devour (1 Peter 5:8).

"You belong to your father, the devil, and you want to carry out your father's desire. He was a murderer from the beginning, not holding to the truth, for there is no truth in him" (John 8:44).

Scripture reveals that Satan is the lawless one, the enemy, and a thief who seeks to kill, lie, steal, and destroy. Yet, he pretends to be an angel of light. Sometimes he goes around in a threatening manner like a lion seeking to destroy. However, we have weapons for opposing Satan and his devises. Paul counseled the Ephesians to put on the armor of God.

Read Ephesians 6:10-18 in your Bible, and list the spiritual weapons available to us.

• belt of _____ around your waist
• breastplate of _____
• feet filled with the gospel of _____
• shield of _____
• helmet of _____
• sword of the _____

Decide now to resist any spiritual attack with the Word of God. Christ defeated Satan in the wilderness by speaking God's Word (see Matthew 4:1-11). Study and memorize the Word. You are more than a conqueror in Jesus Christ.

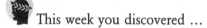 Say the following passages silently or out loud as a closing prayer and declaration of your victory in Jesus Christ.

"I am convinced that neither death nor life, neither angels nor demons, neither the present nor the future, nor any powers, neither height nor depth, nor anything else in all creation, will be able to separate [me] from the love of God that is in Christ Jesus" (Romans 8:38-39).

The Bottom Line
- **The attacks of Satan are a powerful storm that every Christian must face.**
- **We have weapons for opposing Satan and his devises.**
- **Decide now to resist any spiritual attack with the Word of God.**

This week you discovered ...
- you have a responsibility to serve God and counter the attacks of Satan.
- you will be involved in spiritual warfare.
- how to resist any spiritual attack through your faith in Jesus Christ.

What does God want you to do in response to this week's study?

Recite Joshua 1:8 as a closing thought for the week.

TRUE SUCCESS

Any man who says he doesn't want to be successful is a liar or a fool or both. The only issue is, "What is *true* success?"

In one sense, this entire series on *The Seven Seasons of a Man's Life* is about success. Each season points us to the Season of Success.

What is *true* success? Can any man be considered truly successful who does not have an assurance that when he dies he will go to heaven? I think not. The Bible asks, "What can be compared with the value of eternal life?" (Matthew 16:26, TLB). No matter how many good deeds you perform, accolades you receive, poor people you feed, or how much money you give to the church, unless you have asked Jesus to forgive your sins and trusted Him to be your Savior and Lord, you are no success.

Conversely, can any man be considered a failure if he knows Christ? Actually, yes. Even though you succeed *spiritually* (you have the assurance of eternal life), you can still fail *morally* (living without integrity), *relationally* (failing to love others as Christ commands), or *financially* (failing to provide for your family). You may go to heaven, but ignominiously: "He himself will be saved, but only as one escaping through the flames" (1 Corinthians 3:15). To fail to live a life of love, faith, obedience, and service in your marriage, family, work, church, and community is to build with "wood, hay or straw" (1 Corinthians 3:12).

In the Season of Success, we have identified four essential attitudes of successful Christian men. This week we will …

• Seek to understand how God defines true success.
• Consider our next steps in maturing in Christ toward the level of success He desires in our lives.
• Ask questions of where we go from here.

★ DAY 1 ★
Refocusing
Priorities

★ DAY 2 ★
The Success
Quiz

★ DAY 3 ★
What Makes
a Real Man?

★ DAY 4 ★
Success in
the Public
Square

★ DAY 5 ★
Leave the
World
Better Than
You Found it

As you examine your attitudes about success and where you find yourself as a successful man in Jesus Christ, I pray that God's Spirit will give you wisdom and understanding. God wills for you to prosper and be successful in all you do for His glory. This verse is my prayer for you this week. In turn, make it your prayer for others.

Dear friend, I pray that you may enjoy good health and that all may go well with you, even as your soul is getting along well (3 John 2).

REFOCUSING PRIORITIES

When I opened the morning paper, I was stung by the headline. One of our city's most prominent businessmen was dead. For several days shock waves rippled through our business community. Everyone was stunned as details became available about the tragic airplane crash that took the life of such a big player.

That was about 10 years ago. I must tell you that today no one misses the man. In fact, since his funeral, I have heard his name mentioned only one time. You see, his death was shocking but not tragic. His prominence created a shock, but because he had invested only in *things* rather than in *people,* hardly anyone was saddened by his death. In other words, he was commercially successful but relationally poor. He was a man who lived only for his own self-interests. He did not invest in other people. Everything he did, he did for himself.

There are many ways to measure success. First and foremost, it is measured spiritually by our relationship with Jesus Christ as Lord and Savior. Then, other areas of success surface—moral, relational, and financial success.

My brother-in-law was offered a lucrative job with a major software company. But the job meant a great deal of travel, taking him away from his family and children.

He turned down the offer. Certainly, he wanted to advance his career and make more money. Who doesn't? But he didn't let his personal ambition detour him from his calling. He understood a few key principles we have already discussed that we will review. As has already been said, the problem for many men is not so much that they are failing. Rather, the problem is they are achieving the wrong goals.

Failure sometimes means to succeed in a way that doesn't really matter. There are many ways to measure success beyond career success. No amount of success at work will compensate for failure at home. To succeed in your career but fail at home is to fail completely.

◆

True success is to satisfy your *calling*, not your *ambition*.

In light of what you've learned by evaluating yourself through the activities in this book, complete the following sentence: God's purpose, vision, plan, or calling on my life is to...

_____

_____

How are you maturing toward God's call and purpose in your life?

Unless we remain vigilant to "take captive every thought to make it obedient to Christ" (2 Corinthians 10:5), we become products, even prisoners, of our own culture. Once culture-bound to a man-centered world, we tend to evaluate (read: e-*value*-ate) how we are doing on the basis of the world's default values.

Here is a list of worldly values that measure man's success. Check the values by which you have measured your self-worth.

❑ performance	❑ production	❑ prestige
❑ possessions	❑ perception	❑ status
❑ acceptance	❑ appearance	❑ finances
❑ physical attractiveness	❑ athleticism	❑ happiness
❑ IQ	❑ other:_____	

Our culture offers value only to people who possess the above attributes. Our culture grants human worth to you in proportion to how good you look, how smart you are, how much money you have, and/or how athletic you are.

To be considered successful in the eyes of the world, you are required to display one or more of the four killer "bees": *beauty, brains, bucks,* and *brawn.* If you don't have one of these attributes, forget it. The emphasis is always on externals—what you have and do—rather than on who and Whose you are.

These worldly values can demand our attention and become the measure of our own personal success. Is that true for you? Put an x on the bar to indicate where you are right now in the process of measuring success by externals versus measuring success by the things of God.

Success by   Success measured
worldly externals   by Godly internals

God measures success by what's in our hearts. The Word of God says that as Samuel looked over Jesse's boys to anoint one of them king, God said, "Do not consider his appearance or his height. ... The Lord does not look at the things man looks at. Man looks at the outward appearance, but the Lord looks at the heart" (1 Samuel 16:7).

How *should* we decide how we are doing? The Bible helps us re-focus on those priorities that really count. Answer each of the following questions by marking an x on the bar where you are right now. Is this where you were six months ago? Check the bar where you were six months ago. Are you growing or stagnant?

Am I putting God first in my life? (Matthew 6:33).

I seek first God's   I try to seek   I'm not seeking first
kingdom and   God's kingdom   God's kingdom
character.   and character.   and character.

Am I maintaining my first love, Jesus Christ? (Revelation 2:4).

I'm on fire for Jesus.   I'm lukewarm.   I'm cold in my faith.

Am I in the center of God's will? (Philippians 2:13).

I'm living His will.   I'm seeking His will.   I'm not in His will.

Am I consistently seeking after the will of God? (Romans 12:2).

I consistently seek God's will.	I occasionally seek God's will.	I rarely seek God's will.

Am I the husband, father, and provider I should be? (1 Timothy 5:8).

I am the family man God calls me to be.	I am seeking to grow as a godly family man.	I am not being the family man God calls me to be.

Am I a faithful, diligent, honest employee or employer? (Colossians 3:23-25).

I am fulfilling my calling at work.	I am seeking God's direction in work.	God is not part of my work.

Am I seeking to be financially responsible? (Luke 16:10-12).

I am financially responsible.	I am financially responsible most of the time	I lack financial responsibility.

When men sincerely ask these questions of themselves on a regular basis, they will find a true success that really matters. Decide which area of your life could use the most spiritual growth and cultivation. Write a prayer that asks for God's Spirit to guide and empower you to live for Jesus Christ in this area of your life.

_____

_____

_____

_____

Review today's lesson carefully. What does God want you to do as a result of your study?

_____

_____

_____

The Bottom Line
- To succeed in your career but fail at home is to fail completely.
- True success is to satisfy your *calling*, not your *ambition*.
- Once culture-bound to a man-centered world, we tend to evaluate how we are doing on the basis of the world's default values.
- God measures success by what's in our hearts.

THE SUCCESS QUIZ

Success that really matters means a well-rounded, well-balanced, priority-based, thought-through process.

◆

**God wants Christian men to be successful in
every area of their lives.**

I do not think a man will feel and sense that his life has been successful unless he can honestly answer yes to all these important questions.

Check the column that most fits where you are right now.

	Yes	No	Growing
1. Am I performing fulfilling work?	❑	❑	❑
2. Am I a good provider?	❑	❑	❑
3. Am I doing everything possible to help my children become responsible adults?	❑	❑	❑
4. Am I building a strong, loving marriage?	❑	❑	❑
5. Am I doing everything possible to introduce my family to faith in Christ?	❑	❑	❑
6. Am I investing in other people's lives as a friend, counselor, accountability partner, and mentor?	❑	❑	❑
7. Am I living a life of good deeds?	❑	❑	❑
8. Am I living a life of integrity?	❑	❑	❑
9. Am I walking closely with the Lord Jesus every day?	❑	❑	❑
10. Will I go to heaven when I die?	❑	❑	❑

No matter how poorly you rated yourself, the good news with Christ is that He is the God of redemption. He is a healer, the Great Physician. It's never too late with God. No matter how much of your life you have allowed to slip by without working for true success, He will help you redeem the time.

How does a man get back on track when he has allowed success in one area of life to slip? Choose one of the 10 areas in the previous exercise where you need some work. For each of the following steps, write down a specific action you want to take to move toward godly success.

Repent. Repentance means to change direction. If you are headed in a wrong direction, turn to God and seek His righteousness and holiness. "Godly sorrow brings repentance that leads to salvation and leaves no regret, but worldly sorrow brings death" (2 Corinthians 7:10).

I need to repent of _____

_____

_____

Confess. Confess your sins and failures and accept responsibility for what you have done. "If we confess our sins, he is faithful and just and will forgive us our sins and purify us from all unrighteousness" (1 John 1:9).

I confess that _____

_____

_____

Receive forgiveness. The blood of Christ cleanses us from all sin. Let go of the past and move forward in the grace and forgiveness of Jesus Christ.

I receive forgiveness for _____

_____

_____

Seek the direction of the Holy Spirit and God's Word. Pray for the Holy Spirit to reveal God's truth and to direct your path as you study His Word. "The word of God is living and active. Sharper than any double-edged sword, it penetrates even to dividing soul and spirit, joints and marrow, it judges the thoughts and attitudes of the heart (Hebrews 4:12).

I need to hear God's Word speak to me _____

_____

_____

Be accountable to other Christians. Pray and share with other Christians who will hold you accountable as you walk with the Lord "We who are strong ought to bear with the failings of the weak and not to please ourselves (Romans 15:1).

Other Christians to whom I will be accountable are _____

_____

_____

Seek out mature Christians to disciple and mentor you. Learn from good teachers of the Word and mentors who will disciple you in your walk. "Listen to advice and accept instruction, and in the end you will be wise" (Proverbs 19:20).

My Christian mentors include _____

_____

_____

Consider checking off these steps as you do them. Why not come back in a few weeks and evaluate your progress?

What does God want you to do as a result of today's study?

_____

_____

In closing today, write a prayer to God committing yourself to seeking to be successful in every area of your life.

_____

_____

_____

The Bottom Line
- God wants Christian men to be successful in every area of their lives.
- No matter how much of your life you have allowed to slip by without working for true success, God will help you redeem the time.

WHAT MAKES A REAL MAN?

Despite past failures, it's never too late to become a real man.

◆

**God wants you to be a real man who
reflects the character of Christ.**

I see four qualities that separate the real men from the "wannabees."

Read each of the qualities and suggested Scripture passages. Put an x on each bar to indicate where you are in modeling these qualities. Then identify one step you can take with God's leading to grow in each area.

1. A real man is a man of courage (Joshua 1:6-9). He is not afraid to love his Lord, cherish his wife, nurture his children, be excellent in his work, be faithful in his service, and be vulnerable with his friends. He does all this before a watching world, unashamed.

I am bold and strong   I am timid and afraid.
in the Lord.

One step I could take to take to grow in my boldness is _____

_____

2. A real man is a man of wisdom (James 1:5). He doesn't take himself too seriously. As he gets older, he laughs more. He learns to let little offenses go. In fact, bigger and bigger offenses seem smaller and smaller in his mind. He realizes people are weak, and he himself is far weaker than he once thought. He seeks more advice, and he doesn't always accept the first solution to his problems as the best solution.

I am wise in the   I lack wisdom.
things of God.

One area in my life in which I need wisdom is _____

_____

3. A real man is a man of commitments (Proverbs 8:7). He has consciously decided to set aside his personal, selfish goals and ask how he can live for Christ. He has decided to make the four commitments of a kingdom builder. A kingdom builder commits to *build the kingdom* (the Great Commission in Matthew 28:18-20); *tend the culture* (the Cultural Commission in Genesis 1:28); *love other people* (the New Commandment in John 13:34-35); and *love the King* (the Great Commandment in Matthew 22:37-38).

I speak truth and   I have a difficult time
keep my commitments.   keeping my commitments.

The next step I should take to keep my commitments is _____

_____

4. A real man is a man of balance (Proverbs 4). He loves God without neglecting to serve Him. He cherishes and nurtures his family without neglecting to provide for them. He enjoys each day as a gift from God without neglecting to provide for retirement and the risk of early death. He gives his employer a full day's work without neglecting to save enough energy for the ones who will sit on the front row at his funeral.

I am living a   My life is out
balanced life.   of balance.

The next step I want to take to find balance in my life is _____

_____

_____

Have you been pursuing success that really matters?
❑ yes   ❑ no   ❑ need to improve
How are you doing? How should you be doing?

_____

_____

If you died today, would anyone really care? What changes can you make in your life to find real, biblical success? List those changes.

_____

_____

_____

Read this *Prayer by an Unknown Confederate Soldier.* After you have read it completely, underline one couplet that significantly speaks to you.

I asked God for strength, that I might achieve.
I was made weak, that I might learn humbly to obey.
I asked for health, that I might do greater things.
I was given infirmity, that I might do better things.
I asked for riches, that I might be happy.
I was given poverty, that I might be wise.
I asked for power, that I might have the praise of men.
I was given weakness, that I might feel the need of God.
I asked for all things, that I might enjoy life.
I was given life, that I might enjoy all things.
I got nothing that I asked for—but everything I had hoped for.
Almost despite myself, my unspoken prayers were answered.
I am among all men, most richly blessed.

We can learn much from the unknown soldier. Like us, he prayed for what he thought he wanted. What do we think we want? Strength, health, riches, power—all things. And why do we want it? So that we might achieve, do greater things, be happy, receive the praise of men, and enjoy life.

100

In His kindness God answers the misguided prayer, not with what we want but what we need. Sometimes He gives infirmity, poverty, weakness—but always life. And why? So that we might learn to obey, do better things, be wise, feel the need of God, and enjoy all things.

When we get nothing we ask for, let us be mindful that our great God will give us everything we need and all that we hope for—almost despite ourselves.

Today's lesson contained much to consider. Review it carefully. What is one idea that you would like to thing about more deeply during the next few days?

_____

_____

_____

The Bottom Line
- God wants you to be a real man who reflects the character of Christ.
- A real man is a man of courage.
- A real man is a man of wisdom.
- A real man is a man of commitments.
- A real man is a man of balance.

SUCCESS IN THE PUBLIC SQUARE

We live in an era in which the leavening influence of Christian faith on American society and culture has eroded like a washed-out road. In one generation we have witnessed a catastrophic decline in education, law, government, the arts, entertainment, and every other arena. Simultaneously, we have witnessed a meteoric rise in Christian divorce, sexual perversion, violence, abortion, drug abuse, youth gangs, inner-city despair, and much more. Could anyone deny that, by and large, the church is losing the battle for the culture? Why is this? And where is the compelling draw of a gospel that changes men's lives?

Below is a list of areas where you might influence the culture for Christ. Check areas in which God has stirred you to make a difference.

❑ Government   ❑ The arts
❑ Education   ❑ Entertainment
❑ Family issues   ❑ Abortion issues
❑ Violence, gangs, and crime   ❑ Drug abuse and addiction
❑ Urban problems   ❑ Inner-city despair
❑ Problems associated with pornography

If 60 million people claim to be born again—and they do—then how could this decline of culture possibly take place? Good question. The reason is the problem of Cultural Christianity versus Biblical Christianity. Gallup demonstrated in a recent poll that only 10 percent of Americans are deeply-committed Biblical Christians.

The unhappy result of Cultural Christianity is an impotent, self-centered faith that doesn't change things. In short, Cultural Christians live mostly for themselves and don't invest in the kingdom.

Here is a great problem in the world today:

◆

**Men have overemphasized their private faith
to the detriment of their public duties.**

To be a truly successful man requires you to take responsibility for your private life–your relationships with your wife and children, your finances, health, and walk with God–*and* that you also take responsibility for building the kingdom and tending the culture. Real men will enter the public battle to restore the leavening influence of true Christian faith on the culture.

The irony is that we are there–Christians are everywhere, only silent. Except for a few voices, ours has been a generation uninvolved in the debates taking place on the public square. I'm not suggesting Christian men should try to usher in Christian government, media, or marketplace. But we should be vitally involved in working for government that governs Christianly, media that reports fairly, and a marketplace that competes with integrity.

What can we do? We can say, "I want my life to count."

Mark an x on the bar to indicate your involvement as a Christian in the public arena right now.

Very involved   Not involved

If men across this nation who *know* Christ in *private* will also *live* for Christ in *public*, we can experience a return to sanity. What are you willing to invest?

Check all the things you are willing to do publicly as a Christian witness and servant. Then on the line to the right of the item you checked, describe a specific action you intend to take as a result of this commitment. For instance, if you checked *Become involved in community and civic organizations,* your specific application might be *Coach a little league baseball team in an urban area.*

❏ Serve in local government as a volunteer _____

_____

❏ Get involved in the school system _____

_____

❏ Run for elected office _____

_____

103

❑ Become involved in community and civic organizations _____

_____

❑ Be a volunteer in a community service group _____

_____

❑ Other: _____

_____

Don't let your answer stay in this book—give it life. Don't just write it—
do it. This is my bottom line conclusion: We don't need any more
Christians to win our nation back to God. What we need is for the
Christians we already have to *be* Christian, wherever they are.

Read the following Scripture. Close in prayer, praying the Lord
will show you how to make a difference in the culture in which you live.

"You are the salt of the earth. But if the salt loses it saltiness, how can
it be made salty again? It is no longer good for anything, except to be
thrown out and trampled by men.

"You are the light of the world. A city on a hill cannot be hidden.
Neither do people light a lamp and put it under a bowl. Instead they
put it on its stand, and it gives light to everyone in the house. In the
same way, let your light shine before men, that they may see your good
deeds and praise your Father in heaven" (Matthew 5:13-16).

The Bottom Line
- By and large, the church is losing the battle for the
  culture.
- Men have overemphasized their private faith to the
  detriment of their public duties.
- Real men will enter the public battle to restore the
  leavening influence of true Christian faith on the
  culture.
- If men across the nation who *know* Christ in *private*
  will also *live* for Christ in *public*, we can experience a
  return to sanity.

LEAVE THE WORLD BETTER THAN YOU FOUND IT

Recently, someone shared this. Someone had passed it along to him, and I pass it along to you.

- The world is a better place because Michelangelo didn't say, "I don't do ceilings."
- The world is a better place because Martin Luther didn't say, "I don't do doors."
- The world is a better place because Noah didn't say, "I don't do arks."
- The world is a better place because David didn't say, "I don't do giants."
- The world is a better place because Jeremiah didn't say, "I don't do weeping."
- The world is a better place because Peter didn't say, "I don't do Gentiles."
- The world is a better place because Paul didn't say, "I don't do letters."
- The world is a better place because Mary didn't say, "I don't do virgin births."
- The world is a better place because Jesus didn't say, "I don't do crosses."

◆

God calls real men to leave the world better than they found it.

Will the world be a better place because you didn't say, "I don't do (fill in the blank) _____

What will you put in the blank space? What will be your legacy? Will you discover and answer God's calling, both private and public?

Dwight L. Moody, the Billy Graham of the 19th century, one day heard these challenging words which marked the beginning of a new era in his life: "The world has yet to see what God will do with, and for, and through, and in, and by the man who is fully and wholly consecrated to Him."

"He said 'a man', thought Moody. "He did not say a great man, nor a learned man, nor a rich man, nor a wise man, nor an eloquent man, nor a 'smart' man, but simply 'a man.' I am a man, and it lies with the man himself whether he will, or will not, make that entire and full consecration. I will try my utmost to be that man." [1]

Will you try your utmost to be that man?

One thing I can do with my ...

... **family** that leaves them in a better place is _____

_____

... **church** that leaves it a better place is_____

_____

... **work** that leaves it a better place is _____

_____

... **relationships** that leaves other people in a better place is_____

_____

What is one thing every Christian man can do to make a difference daily in the world? James 5:16 gives us the clue, "The prayer of a righteous man is powerful and effective."

In closing today, write a prayer asking God to help you live a life that will leave the world better than you found it.

_____

_____

The Bottom Line
• God calls real men to leave the world better than they found it.

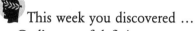 This week you discovered …
• God's way of defining success.
• the next steps you need to take in maturing in Christ toward the level of success He desires in your life.
What does God want you to do in response to this week's study?

_____

_____

Recite 3 John 2 as a closing thought for the week.

---

[1]W.P. Moody, _The Life of Dwight L. Moody_ (Westwood: Barbour and Company, Inc. 1985), 122.

REFLECTING ON THIS SEASON

1. The most important truth I learned for my spiritual life:

_____

_____

2. The Scripture passage that spoke to me with the most meaning (write the scripture or your paraphrase of it):

_____

_____

_____

3. One thing I need to confess to the Lord and ask forgiveness for:

_____

4. One thing I need to praise the Lord for:

_____

5. One important change the Lord and I need to make in my life:

_____

6. The next step I need to take in obedience:

_____

REDEFINING SUFFERING AND SUCCESS

This week we will review the Seasons of Suffering and Success. The world defines suffering and success very differently from the way Christianity defines them. The world scorns suffering and seeks to avoid it at any cost. Christians, on the other hand, embrace the suffering of Jesus Christ on the cross as redeeming them from their sin. Christian men can enter into the suffering of Christ and minister to one another and the needs of a hurting world.

The world sees success from the perspective of the four "killer bees"– *brawn, brains, beauty,* and *bucks.* Biblical Christians, on the other hand, define success by the God-given qualities that come from the heart such as purity, holiness, and righteousness.

During our lifetimes, we will feel the gentle breeze of success and the harsh wind of suffering. We can no more control our seasons than we can control winter, spring, summer, and fall. At the height of financial success, tragedy may strike. In the depth of despair, light breaks through.

Although we can't control our seasons, God gives us the Holy Spirit so that we can control ourselves. We can live lives of integrity, meaning, and worth, fulfilling God's calling and purpose for us. Each of us can grow and mature as the kind of man God will bless and make a blessing to others. In this study, we have sought to show you how to build with "silver, gold, and costly stones" on the only foundation that will survive, the foundation of Jesus Christ and His Word (Matthew 7:24-27; 1 Corinthians 3:11-13).

As we review the biblical definitions of suffering and success, let's seek God's direction and power to be the Christlike men He calls us to be. *Being* God's man precedes *doing* godly deeds. Who and Whose we are in Jesus Christ always form the foundation for what we do as Christian men.

★ DAY 1 ★
The Nature of Suffering

★ DAY 2 ★
Four Consoling Truths About Suffering

★ DAY 3 ★
Four Attitudes of Successful Men (Part 1)

★ DAY 4 ★
Four Attutudes of Successful Men (Part 2)

★ DAY 5 ★
True Success

My prayer is that this week will be an encouragement to you in your seasons of suffering and success. Memorize and meditate on this verse during your review.

Speaking the truth in love, we will in all things grow up into him who is the Head, that is, Christ (Ephesians 4:15).

THE NATURE OF
SUFFERING

During Week 1 of this study, we explored the nature of suffering. Today, let's review the main ideas from that week.

◆

Day 1: Suffering makes us face the deepest questions about our lives.

What is suffering? Is what we call suffering really suffering? We have all agonized over the question, "Why do bad things happen to good or innocent people?"

For most people the issue comes down to two questions: *If God is good, why does He allow situations that cause people to suffer?* and *If God is all-powerful, why doesn't He remove all suffering?*

How would you respond to the statement, "Since there is so much suffering in the world, God must not be good or all-powerful. If He loved humanity, He would not let terrible things happen."

_____

_____

Either God is sovereign or He's not, and either God is good or He's not. Is God sovereign? In control of all things? The unequivocal claim of Scripture is yes. Is God good? All-benevolent? The unequivocal claim of Scripture is yes. Can we fully understand this? No, we cannot. But we can trust Him.

◆

Day 2: God never allows any suffering, pain, or evil to touch us unless it will bring about a greater good or prevent a greater evil.

Every parent has been in circumstances when they watched their children suffer. A parent will do anything possible to make his child's life

111

easier unless in the end it will make his life harder. Sometimes, a parent knows that hard circumstances will result in a greater good in the long run. A truly loving parent has goals for his children that are larger than their immediate sufferings.

As our Heavenly Father, God loves us enough to put the development of our character before the development of our circumstances. As God's children, we need His discipline. We need the suffering He allows to build and strengthen our character. As we become able to endure and overcome difficulties, we become more effective witnesses to His power at work in us.

◆

Day 3: God uses every circumstance to help us mature, develop, and grow.

God does not author evil nor will it. God overcomes evil. Eventually, we see His Hand at work in every circumstance.

We should be cautious about thinking of our hardships as hardships. Rather, what we often think of as suffering is the means of grace to bring us into a closer reliance upon God.

I'm not saying suffering doesn't hurt. I'm not suggesting the pain is not real. Why does a bodybuilder endure pain until his muscles groan for rest? He knows it is the only way he can achieve his goal. In the same way, the Bible says "our light and momentary troubles are achieving for us an eternal glory that far outweighs them all" (2 Corinthians 4:17).

◆

Day 4: The wise man will look beyond his sufferings to the reasons for it.

Here's what real suffering is: To be allowed to completely direct our own lives to our eventual destruction. Tragic suffering results when we rebel and abandon the chastening that comes from a loving Father.

We may suffer for one of three reasons: 1) for doing wrong, 2) for doing right, or 3) for no apparent reason. If we are suffering the consequences of a wrong decision and God is chastening and correcting, we must submit to the blows of His loving correction. On the other hand, if we are going through a season of suffering because we stood up for right, we can be glad.

Sometimes, our sufferings seem to be without reason or logic. Perhaps the hardest sufferings to understand are the seemingly random acts of pain that befall us all from time to time. In such situations we must submit ourselves to the mercy of God and continue to do good.

◆

Day 5: Suffering is not just a test, it is also a blessing.

Ask God to teach you every lesson He intends for you during your hard time, lest you have to travel that road again. Suffering will make us bitter or better. The choice is ours.

Suffering is a gift from God to refine our faith and give us the privilege of sharing with Christ in His suffering. I have paraphrased 1 Peter 1:6-7 replacing "you" with "I". Read this passage as a prayer, rejoicing in Christ's suffering so God might use you for His purposes.

In this I greatly rejoice, though now for a little while I may have had to suffer grief in all kinds of trials. These have come so that my faith—of greater worth than gold, which perishes even though refined by fire—may be proved genuine and may result in praise, glory and honor when Jesus Christ is revealed.

Throughout the study I have provided a summary of each day's material called "The Bottom Line." During these last five days, I want you to create your own "bottom line." What one truth has been most meaningful to you during each week of your study? At the end of each day this week, you will have an opportunity to write that truth. Reflect on what has been important to you. Ask God to help you live that truth each day.

The Bottom Line

_____

_____

FOUR CONSOLING TRUTHS ABOUT SUFFERING

Life simultaneously chugs along two tracks: the track of joy and the track of suffering. We frequently find ourselves immersed in joy and sorrow at the same time. In the midst of this paradox, we can know certain truths about suffering. During week 2, we studied four consoling truths about suffering. Let's review the big ideas of that week.

◆

Day 1: Every man experiences seasons of suffering throughout his life.

God brings suffering in and out of our lives at times of His choosing. This suffering draws us back to Him. God uses it to take our trust in Him from abstract and theoretical to personal and concrete. The truths of God's Word sustain us in this suffering and help us draw near to God.

◆

Day 2: There is nothing you can do to avoid suffering in this life.

Suffering is certain. In this world you will suffer.

Some men believe that by careful planning they can avoid pain and suffering. We can spend enormous amounts of time, money, and energy to avoid inconvenience and suffering. These efforts are futile. No matter where we are, we will suffer.

◆

Day 3: Today's Christian culture calls us to comfort, the Bible calls us to suffer.

In our contemporary world, our suffering presents us with two choices. First, we can join in the crusade to shape the world into a utopia by seeking to eliminate all sources of potential pain. Or, second, we can accept that the "world in its present form is passing away" (1 Corinthians 7:31) and enter into the Bible's call to suffer.

The call to suffer is at its simplest the call to follow Jesus Christ. Because He suffered, we too will suffer.

The following verses teach us about the Christian's call to suffer. Put your initials beside the one that seems most applicable to your past or present circumstances.

"To this you were called, because Christ suffered for you, leaving you an example, that you should follow in his steps" (1 Peter 2:21).

"We must go through many hardships to enter the kingdom of God" (Acts 14:22).

"Consider it pure joy, my brothers, whenever you face trials of many kinds" (James 1:2).

"In fact, everyone who wants to live a godly life in Christ Jesus will be persecuted" (2 Timothy 3:12).

"If you are insulted because of the name of Christ, you are blessed, for the Spirit of glory and of God rests on you" (1 Peter 4:14).

What makes the verse that you initialed so meaningful to you?

_____

_____

◆

Day 4: There is no such thing as meaningless suffering.

The Bible tells us that there is purpose to suffering. Jesus suffered to redeem us from sin and death. We suffer with Christ to accomplish His eternal, spiritual purposes. God puts things in front of us that are bigger than we are so we must depend upon Him.

The Bible doesn't always give us a precise answer to a particular situation. At that point we decide by faith to accept the mystery in the nature of God. The one question we cannot answer is, "Why is there suffering at all?" We don't know. "The secret things belong to the Lord our God" (Deuteronomy 29:29). But this we do know: God is good.

115

◆

**Day 5: Because there is purpose to suffering,
there is comfort in suffering.**

Through our suffering, God corrects our faulty thinking, spares us from greater evils, and brings about greater goods. God leads us to repent of our sins and produces in us the character of His Son, Jesus.

"Praise be to the God and Father of our Lord Jesus Christ, the Father of compassion and the God of all comfort, who comforts us in all our troubles, so that we can comfort those in any trouble with the comfort we ourselves have received from God" (2 Corinthians 1:3-4).

In closing today, write a prayer to God asking for discernment during times of suffering.

_____

_____

The Bottom Line

_____

_____

FOUR ATTITUDES OF SUCCESSFUL MEN (PART 1)

During week 3 of our study, we examined two attitudes of successful men. Using the life of David as a starting point, we looked at how we can be truly successful in the way God defines success.

◆

**Day 1: The key to our success is to be
"a man after God's own heart."**

No man in the Bible ever received more approval from God than David. No man represents a better model for how we should live our lives. The greatest thing we could hope for is to be called a man after God's own heart. God doesn't seek perfection, but rather a willing, compliant heart.

◆

Day 2: A successful man will take risks for God.

No one else would go out to fight against Goliath, but David risked almost certain death and went. When everyone else's courage melted, David did not lose heart.

Like David, we should take more risks, but not without some calculation and preparation. Success is that point at which preparation meets opportunity.

We will only take risks when we stand firm on God's truth and strength. Many people never attempt anything significant because they might fail. We should take calculated risks because we believe God is able to complete what He put in our hearts to do.

◆

**Day 3: Courage is not the absence of fear but a willingness
to trust God in the presence of fear.**

Hudson Taylor said, "Many Christians estimate difficulties in light of their own resources, and thus attempt little and often fail in the little they do attempt. All God's giants have been weak men who did great things for God because they reckoned on His power and presence being with them."

Over and over again in Scripture, God's messengers tell them to whom they are sent, "Fear not." We can be courageous because we know God is on our side. God's presence in our lives is the wellspring that brings forth courage.

◆

Day 4: So, closely identify everything you do with God that before men can prevail against you, they must first prevail against God.

King Asa of Judah was a relentless reformer. He cleaned up the nation and made laws that required people to obey God's commandments. What did he get for his troubles? An army of one million troops marched against him.

Asa responded, "Lord, there is no one like you to help the powerless against the mighty. Help us, O Lord our God, for we rely on you, and in your name we have come against this vast army. O Lord, you are our God; do not let man prevail against you" (2 Chronicles 14:11). To paraphrase Asa, "they can't whip us until they finish whipping God."

Dependence on God is the only way to achieve godly success. When we succeed in our own strength, our egos swell up in pride and the achievement only lasts for a brief time. When God accomplishes His plans through us, the results are lasting and eternal.

◆

Day 5: True success is a by-product of complete dependence on Jesus Christ.

The man who depends on his own strength or trusts in the value system of this world will be miserable. The independent man is never able to satisfy his thirst for significance and purpose. We all know men who live in opulence, yet their creased faces betray a life of independence lived in parched places.

The difference between the man who trusts in God and the man who trusts in himself is not in the circumstances, but in his response. The man who trusts God knows that hard times will come, but he does not fear them.

We are not independent, self-sustaining beings; we depend on God for health, provision, circumstances, and the future. A man will only find true success as he lives in daily, step-by-step dependence on God.

Are you convinced these attitudes can help you be a successful man? Rate your agreement by marking an x on the following bars.

| I still feel like | I am willing to take |
| I need to play it safe. | some risks for God. |

| I have a hard time not | I am committed to relying |
| depending on myself | on God alone. |

If you are not satisfied with your responses, talk with God and seek His guidance. Close your study today in prayer to God.

The Bottom Line

_____

_____

FOUR ATTITUDES OF SUCCESSFUL MEN (PART 2)

During week 4 of our study, we examined two more attitudes of successful men. Let's review and reexamine the big ideas from that week.

◆

Day 1: You must take personal responsibility for the outcome of your life.

When David went out to fight Goliath, he depended completely on God. But it wasn't God who hurled the stone or cut off Goliath's head–David did. We could put it this way:

• Success is the result of God's blessing, not man's effort.
• Success does not depend on man's effort, but rarely comes without hard work.

Working hard will not guarantee success, but not working hard will guarantee failure. Unfortunately, success does not always come in direct proportion to the amount of effort we put forth, but failure usually comes in direct proportion to our laziness. God is not calling men to be successful; He is calling men to be faithful.

◆

Day 2: A successful man will take responsibility to obey God's Word.

The Bible gives men clear direction about their attitudes and behaviors. We must take responsibility to learn what the Bible teaches and then seek to obey out of a loving relationship with God.

True success is not determined by our abilities, but by our humble availability to be used by God. When we obey God's Word, we become servants of Christ whom God can use to accomplish His purpose in the world.

◆

Day 3: The successful man expects opposition, even when he is doing God's will.

The problem with life is that there is opposition. Often, great opportunity is accompanied by great opposition.

If you expect opposition, you will be prepared for it when it happens. You can avoid the negative feelings that may arise, and you can learn to respond to resistance in a godly manner.

◆

Day 4: Opposition comes from within, from the world, from hypocrites, and from Satan.

The first step in facing real opposition is to determine where the attack is coming from. We experience attack from within when our sinful nature (flesh) attacks our spiritual nature. We experience attack from the world when we are tempted by our culture to do things for our own pleasure and self-serving motives. Religious hypocrites attack and criticize God's purpose for our lives with tradition, legalism, and self-righteousness. Satan attacks us with spiritual warfare whenever a man is trying to follow Christ.

◆

Day 5: The attacks of Satan are a powerful storm that every Christian must face.

As you try to live out God's calling on your life, you can be sure storms will come. It's important as Christian men that we understand how Satan attacks and how we can withstand his assault.

In Ephesians 6:10-18, Paul lists the weapons that are available to us to defend against Satan's attacks. We have God's truth, the righteousness of Christ, peace that comes from the gospel, our faith in God, the certainty of our salvation, the presence of the Holy Spirit, and the Word of God. When we "put on this armor," we prepare ourselves to resist any spiritual attack.

Are you convinced these attitudes can help you be a successful man? Rate your agreement by marking an x on the following bars.

It is too difficult for me   I am going to
to take responsibility for   take responsibility
for my life right now.   for my life.

I am still surprised   I have learned to
by opposition.   except opposition.

If you are not satisfied with your responses, talk with God and seek His counsel. Close today's review in prayer to God.

The Bottom Line

_____

_____

TRUE SUCCESS

Any man who says he doesn't want to be successful is a liar or a fool or both. The only issue is, "What is true success?" We examined some answers to this question during week 5 of our study. Let's review and re-examine the big ideas from that week.

◆

Day 1: True success is to satisfy your *calling*, not your *ambition*.

The problem for many men is not so much that they are failing. Rather, the problem is they are achieving the wrong goals. Failure means to succeed in a way that doesn't really matter. There are many ways to measure success beyond career success. For example, no amount of success at work will compensate for failure at home.

To be successful in the eyes of the world, you are required to display one or more of the four killer "bees": *beauty, brains, bucks,* and *brawn*. The emphasis is on externals—what you have and do—rather than on who you are.

God measures success by what is in our hearts. "Man looks at the outward appearance, but the Lord looks at the heart" (1 Samuel 16:7).

◆

**Day 2: God wants Christian men to be successful
in every area of their lives.**

Success that really matters comes from a well-rounded, well-balanced, priority-based, thought-through life.

Last week, you answered 10 important questions (page 94) that can help define success. Then you wrote down some steps you could take to move forward in one of these areas. Have you implemented any of these steps? What changes have you seen so far?

123

What changes do you hope to see in the future?

◆

Day 3: God wants you to be a real man who reflects the character of Christ.

A real man is a man of courage (Joshua 1:6-9). A real man is a man of wisdom (James 1:5). A real man is a man of commitments (Proverbs 8:7). A real man is a man of balance (Proverbs 4).

◆

Day 4: Men have overemphasized their private faith to the detriment of their public duties.

We live in an era in which the leavening influence of Christian faith on America society and culture has eroded like a washed-out road. The problem is that we have a large number of Cultural Christians who don't invest in the Kingdom.

The irony is that Christians are everywhere—only silent. Except for a few voices, ours has been a generation uninvolved in the debates taking place on the public square. We should be vitally involved in working for government that governs Christianly, media that reports fairly, and a marketplace that competes with integrity.

If men across this nation who *know* Christ in *private* will also *live* for Christ in *public*, we can experience a return to sanity.

◆

Day 5: God calls real men to leave the world better than they found it.

God has a unique calling on the life of every man. One thing is for sure though, whatever God's calling on your life, He wants you to have an impact on those around you.

Now that you have reviewed what you studied about success, what do you think is at the heart of true success? In two or three sentences, write your definition of true success at the top of the next page.

_____

_____

_____

The Bottom Line

_____

_____

As you go from this study back into the seasons of your life, remember God has a purpose for your life, a calling. God has put you in whatever position you occupy for a reason. God wants you to go into your arena—whether business, the trades, government, education, medicine, law, the arts, entertainment, sports, the military, science, or Christian service—and be a witness for Him among the idols of the world, to *build the kingdom* and *tend the culture*. Go into your arena and be faithful there, whether or not you achieve worldly success. Use your skill, cling to your integrity, and do not be ashamed of your faith.

What now? If you have not studied the other books in *The Seven Seasons of a Man's Life* collection, I encourage you to do so. The back cover of this book provides information to guide you in your selection.

As you turn now to that unique set of problems and opportunities that only you face, know you are not alone, for God makes the seasons.

LEADER GUIDE

In the next six weeks, you will be exploring *The Seasons of Suffering and Success* with a group of men. This leader guide is appropriate for home groups, men's Bible study groups, accountability groups, discipleship and prayer groups, and one-to-one discipling.

The Introductory Session is 90 minutes; weekly sessions are 50 minutes. Consider these suggestions for each session.

Opening Time–This can be a time of sharing and getting caught up on what's happened during the week. Each session has a suggested exercise for this opening time.

Study and Sharing Time–Key exercises and questions for discussion and sharing are provided. Exercises are taken from the weekly material with a page reference usually given. As your group focuses on the material for the week, you may discover that one or more issues will require more time. Do not be discouraged if the group does not cover all the material. The important thing is to discuss what the men in your group *need* to discuss.

Prayer and Closing Time–This is a time for men to pray together corporately or in pairs and to consider "next steps" in their spiritual walks with the Lord.

Each session needs a facilitator; it may be the same person or a different person for each session.

Before each group session the facilitator should:
• Pray for each group member.
• Complete all daily studies for that week.
• Encourage members to complete their work.
• Make handouts of the session material for those who want a separate copy, who forget their book, or who are new to the group.
• Contact members who were absent the last session.

Before the *first* group session, the facilitator should complete Week 1 of the material so he can speak from experience on how he set aside time daily to study.

INTRODUCTORY SESSION

The first group session of *The Seasons of Suffering and Success* is a time of distributing the book, reviewing the material, and understanding the format for the group sessions. This session includes a video presentation by Patrick Morley. Each man should have a copy of the video listening sheet provided in the Administrative Guide.

During the Session

1. Each man introduces himself and takes one minute to tell about himself and his family. (15 minutes)
2. Each man shares one expectation he has of the group and why he came to the group. (10 minutes)
3. Show the video featuring Patrick Morley's challenge and overview of *The Seasons of Suffering and Success.* (40 minutes)
4. Give each man a copy of the book. Explain that a commitment needs to be made to read the daily study and complete all the exercises. Each daily study will take 20 to 30 minutes. (5 minutes)
5. As a group, look at Week 1, Day 1. Have everyone glance over the material and answer any questions they may have about how to use it. (5 minutes)
6. Ask for prayer requests. Repeat the prayer requests, and pray that God's Spirit will guide each man as he studies during the coming week. (10 minutes)
7. Remind each man to complete Week 1 before the next session and to bring his book to every group session. Announce the day, time, and place for the next session. (5 minutes)

Session 1: The Nature of Suffering

Before the Session

- Each man should have completed Week 1.
- This week's facilitator should make copies of this sheet for anyone who wants an extra copy, who may forget his book, or who is new to the group.
- Pray for each person in the group and for the session, asking for God's wisdom and guidance.

During the Session

Opening Time (5-7 minutes)

1. Greet each other as you arrive.
2. Have a man read Philippians 4:12-13 to the group. Ask each man to complete one of these sentences:

   - One area of my live in which I have found true contentment is…
   - One situation in my life that is a source of struggle and hardship for me right now is…

Describe what you believe God may be doing through one of the "bump pains" in your life.

5. God uses hardship to liberate us from sin and bring about our salvation. Have two men read the following passages. As they do, write the redemption God brings out of suffering. Discuss these as a group.

   Romans 8:20-21 ______________________________

   2 Corinthians 12:9-10______________________________

6. God can use suffering to discipline, correct, and strengthen our lives. Share with a partner some of the lessons you have learned from suffering.

7. Here's what real suffering is: To be allowed to completely direct our lives to our eventual destruction. We may suffer for one or more of three reasons:
   - for doing wrong
   - for doing right
   - for no apparent reason

Share with a partner the one area of suffering you are experiencing and how you are handling it. Share what you believe the source of your suffering to be.

3. Individually choose the two or three most common questions you have about suffering. Discuss as a group how you have answered the questions in the past.

- ☐ Exactly what is suffering?
- ☐ Is suffering inevitable?
- ☐ Why do innocent people suffer?
- ☐ What causes suffering?
- ☐ Does there have to be suffering at all?

4. Pain is often God's warning system. God invented "bump pain" to warn us that harder blows will create even more pain (see page 15). Have each man share with the group the most common "bump pains" he experiences. Use the following list.

Check the "bump pains" you have experienced recently.

- ☐ Overdrawn checking account
- ☐ Correction or criticism of someone you respect
- ☐ Argument or correction from your wife
- ☐ Withdrawal by a child
- ☐ Credit rejection
- ☐ Less than positive evaluation at work
- ☐ Speeding ticket
- ☐ Moodiness or outbursts of anger

them as a total group.

- ◆ Suffering makes us face the deepest questions about our lives.
- ◆ God never allows any suffering, pain, or evil to touch us unless it will bring about a greater good or prevent a greater evil.
- ◆ God uses every circumstance to help us mature, develop, and grow.
- ◆ The wise man will look beyond his suffering to the reasons for it.
- ◆ Suffering is not just a test, it is also a blessing.

Prayer and Closing Time (5 minutes)

9. As partners, pray for one another. Ask God to give your partner the wisdom to understand, the ability to accept, the patience to endure, and the power to overcome the difficulty he is now facing.

Session 2: Four Consoling Truths about Suffering

Before the Session

- Each man should have completed Week 2.
- This week's facilitator should make copies of this sheet for anyone who wants an extra copy, who may forget his book, or who is new to the group.
- Pray for each person in the group and for the session, asking for God's wisdom and guidance.

During the Session

Opening Time (5-7 minutes)

1. Greet each other as you arrive.
2. Go around the group with each man sharing:
   - One person who comforted me in a time of pain in my life is...
   - The way he or she comforted me was to...

Study and Sharing Time (35-40 minutes)

3. Review with a partner the four consoling truths about suffering identified in this week's study.
4. We experience various difficulties and times of suffering

---

f. The tragic death of my younger brother.
The death of _____ affected me most and I...

g. Four years of *crisis, business troubles* and *fear of failure* from the Tax Reform Act of 1986.
Crises and fear of failure were from my... _____

5. When you suffer for Christ's sake, what purpose does it serve? Check the one that seems most relevant to your life right now.

☐ That we may be delivered from bondage and become children of God (Romans 8:20-21)

☐ That we will rely on God, not ourselves (2 Corinthians 1:9)

☐ That we may be made more sensitive to others, that we can comfort them with the comfort we ourselves have received (2 Corinthians 1:4; Luke 22:31-33)

☐ That through our sufferings, the saving grace of God will reach more people (2 Corinthians 4:15)

☐ That Christ may receive praise (1 Peter 1:6-7)

☐ That evil may be punished (Deuteronomy 9:4-5)

☐ That we may draw closer to God (2 Corinthians 1:44)

☐ That we will be disciplined (Hebrews 12:5-11)

☐ That our character may be developed (Romans 5:3-5)

...im through that time of suffering.

a. The period of *disillusionment* and *lack of meaning* that led me to drop out of high school.

A period of disillusionment and lack of meaning led me to...

b. A prolonged time of *loneliness* and *emptiness* while in the army.

A period of loneliness and emptiness came when I...

c. The *despair* early in my marriage, which resulted in my surrendering my life to Christ.

A period of despair resulted in my... _____

d. Six months of depressed feelings from *unmet* business expectations and *financial pressure* early in my business career.

My depressed feelings and unmet expectations in _____ led to... _____

e. Pain from migraine headaches, which deeply *discouraged* me.

I became most discouraged when... _____

---

in question 5. Share a personal time of suffering and the reasons that were behind your suffering.

7. Listed below are the BIG IDEAS for the week. Review them as a total group.

- Every man experiences seasons of suffering through-out his life.
- There is nothing you can do to avoid suffering in this life.
- Today's Christian culture calls us to comfort, the Bible calls us to suffer.
- There is no such thing as a meaningless suffering.
- Because there is purpose *to* suffering, there is comfort *in* suffering.

Prayer and Closing Time (5 minutes)

8. With a partner, turn to pages 35-36 in this study guide. Take Psalm 91 and put your partner's name in the blanks. Pray Psalm 91 out loud for your partner.

🐷 Session 3: Four Attitudes of Successful Men (Part 1)

Before the Session

- Each man should have completed Week 3.
- This week's facilitator should make copies of this sheet for anyone who wants an extra copy, who may forget his book, or who is new to the group.
- Pray for each person in the group and for the session, asking for God's wisdom and guidance.

During the Session

Opening Time (5-7 minutes)

1. Greet each other as you arrive.

2. David is called a man after God's own heart. "I [God] have found David son of Jesse a man after my own heart: he will do everything I [God] want him to do" (Acts 13:22). Refer to pages 51-52 for a list of passages about the heart. Have each man share with the group which heart attitude identified in these passages he most desires to grow in his life.

6. The second essential attitude for successful men is *depend on God*. Share with your partner how you shaded the bars of dependence on God on page 63. Pray for each other for the courage to surrender to complete dependence on God.

7. As a total group discuss the differences between a self-help gospel and complete dependence on God. Share as a group the greatest temptations each man faces from the self-help gospel. Use the following comparison list as a basis for your discussion.

Trust in Man	Trust in God
Self-help	Ushering in the Kingdom
Personal fulfillment	Pleasing God
To be something	To be used by God
Guidance	God
Support	Salvation
Help	Holiness
My Will	God's will
"Jesus belongs to me."	"I belong to Jesus."
Christ exists for the sake of man	Man exists for the sake of Christ

3. This week we considered two attitudes of successful men. The first attitude is *take some risks*. Invite any men who are willing to do so to share with the group a significant risk they took for the Lord in their lives and how it turned out.

4. One of the great hindrances to taking risks in our lives is fear. With a partner, share the most common fear you have.

5. Do you have great fears that paralyze your God-given ability to take risks? Here are some common fears of men. Check those that you experience on a regular basis. Share what you checked with your partner.

☐ job loss
☐ marriage dissolving
☐ rebellious child
☐ not being good enough for God
☐ rejection
☐ ridicule
☐ criticism
☐ going to hell
☐ financial loss
☐ other: _____

them as a total group.

◆ The key to our success is to be "a man after God's own heart."
◆ A successful man will take risks for God.
◆ Courage is not the absence of fear but a willingness to trust God in the presence of fear.
◆ So, closely identify everything you do with God that before men can prevail against you, they must first prevail against God.
◆ True success is a by-product of complete dependence on Jesus Christ.

Prayer and Closing Time (5 minutes)

9. As a total group, give each man the opportunity to offer a sentence prayer by completing this sentence:

• Lord, give us the courage to take risks for you in ...

Session 4: Four Attitudes of a Successful Man (Part 2)

Before the Session

- Each man should have completed Week 4.
- This week's facilitator should make copies of this sheet for anyone who wants an extra copy, who may forget his book, or who is new to the group.
- Pray for each person in the group and for the session, asking for God's wisdom and guidance.

During the Session

Opening Time (5-7 minutes)

1. Greet each other as you arrive.
2. Review briefly the first two attitudes of a successful man: take risks and depend on God.

Study and Sharing Time (35-40 minutes)

3. The third attitude of a successful man is to *take responsibility*. Divide into pairs and share how effectively you are taking responsibility.

Humble				Proud
Hungering and thirsting for righteousness				Self-righteous
Merciful				Judgmental
Pure in heart				My own agendas
Peacemaker				Contentious
Happy in persecution				Resentful of persecution

Get with a partner and answer the following question.

- Which area do I need to develop most in my life right now? Why?

6. The fourth attitude we need as successful men is *expect opposition*. As a total group, complete the following sentences:

- Most of the present opposition to righteousness in my life comes from...
- I am preparing myself spiritually to face it by...

them as a total group.

- You must take personal responsibility for the outcome of your life.
- A successful man will take responsibility to obey God's Word.
- The successful man expects opposition, even when he is doing God's will.
- Opposition comes from within, from the world, from hypocrites, and from Satan.
- The attacks of Satan are a powerful storm that every Christian must face.

Prayer and Closing Time (5 minutes)

8. If your group feels comfortable doing this, form a circle and join hands. Ask each man to pray out loud for the man on his right. Choose one aspect of the armor of God (Ephesians 6) to pray for in that man's life. For example, "Lord, I ask for you to give Bill the helmet of salvation so that his every thought will come from you." Start with the group leader and pray clockwise around the circle.

React defensively to criticism

Learn from criticism

[bar scale]

Admit when I'm wrong

Make excuses

[bar scale]

Take the first step in reconciliation and forgiveness

Expect others to take the first step

[bar scale]

4. As a group, review the biblical passages on page 70 about responsibility. Have volunteers share which passage meant the most to them and why.

5. Individually mark an x on the following bars to indicate where you are in living the Beatitudes in Matthew 5.

[bar scale]

Spiritually recognize my need for God

Spiritually arrogant

[bar scale]

Broken hearted by what breaks God's heart

Insensitive to needs

Session 5: True Success

Before the Session

- Each man should have completed Week 5.
- This week's facilitator should make copies of this sheet for anyone who wants an extra copy, who may forget his book, or who is new to the group.
- Pray for each person in the group and for the session.

During the Session

Opening Time (5-7 minutes)
1. Greet each other as you arrive.
2. True success is to satisfy your calling, not your ambition. As a total group, have volunteers share:
   - God's purpose, vision, plan, or calling on my life is to...
   - I (agree or disagree) with the definitions of failure and true success presented in the material because...

Study and Sharing Time (35-40 minutes)
3. In measuring success by God's standards, we need to identify those qualities that make up Godly success. Go around the group and share which qualities each man believes to be important.

- **A real man is a man of wisdom (James 1:5).**

I am wise in the   I lack wisdom.
things of God.

One area in my life in which I need wisdom is _____

- **A real man is a man of commitments (Proverbs 8:7).**

I speak truth and   I have a difficult time
keep my commitments.   keeping my commitments.

The next step I need to take in personal integrity is _____

- **A real man is a man of balance (Proverbs 4).**

I seek first God's kingdom and   My priorities are
have godly priorities   out of balance

The next step I need to take in ordering my priorities is _____

and Whose we are instead of measuring success by what we do. Check the three that are most important to you in measuring biblical success.

___ Uprightness (righteousness)   ___ Integrity
___ Trustworthiness; trusting Jesus   ___ Holiness
___ Love and forgiveness   ___ Purity
___ Obedience to God's Word   ___ Glorifying God

5. We identified four characteristics of a "real man" who is successful in the Lord. Read each one of these characteristics and put an x on the bar to indicate where you are right now. Then identify one step you need to take with God's leading to grow in this area. When you finish, find a partner and share your responses with each other. If you need to review the definition of each characteristic, see pages 98-99.

• A real man is a man of courage (Joshua 1:6-9).

I am bold and strong   I am timid and afraid.
in the Lord.

One step I need to take to grow in my boldness is _____

difference in their world. Ask each man to complete this sentence:

• One way I want to make a difference in my world for Jesus Christ is...

7. Listed below are the BIG IDEAS for the week. Review them as a total group.

♦ True success is to satisfy your *calling*, not your *ambition*.

♦ God wants Christian men to be successful in every area of their lives.

♦ God wants you to be a real man who reflects the character of Christ.

♦ Men have overemphasized their private faith to the detriment of their public duties.

♦ God calls real men to leave the world better than they found it.

Prayer and Closing Time (5 minutes)

8. Ask for personal prayer requests. Pray for each request and close by praying the following prayer in unison:

Almighty God, empower me to be a successful man for your glory and honor that I might make a difference in the world for Jesus Christ. I ask this in Jesus' name, Amen.

Session 6: Redefining Suffering and Success

Before the Session

- Each man should have completed Week 6.
- This week's facilitator should make copies of this sheet for anyone who wants an extra copy, who may forget his book, or who is new to the group.
- Pray for each person in the group and for the session, asking for God's wisdom and guidance.

During the Session

Opening Time (5-7 minutes)

1. Greet each other as you arrive.
2. Have one man read Philippians 3:10 to the group. Ask for a volunteer to share what this verse means to him.

Study and Sharing Time (35-40 minutes)

3. Today's session is a season of reflection on suffering and success. Begin as a group by defining *biblical suffering*. Once you have a definition, individually look over the following Scriptures and circle the one that has become the most meaningful to you over the past few weeks.

"If you are insulted because of the name of Christ, you are blessed, for the Spirit of glory and of God rests on you" (1 Peter 4:14).

What is most meaningful to you about the verse you circled? _____

_____

Share your verse and response to the above question with one other man in the group.

4. As a total group, answer these questions:
   - What types of suffering are most difficult for you personally to understand or accept?
   - How can we accept suffering we do not understand as Christian men?
   - What has God taught you about suffering during this study that has changed your life?

5. We need to have four attitudes as successful men.
   Attitude #1: Take risks.
   Attitude #2: Depend on God.
   Attitude #3: Take responsibility.
   Attitude #4: Expect opposition.

only to believe on him, but also to suffer for him" (Philippians 1:29).

"To this you were called, because Christ suffered for you, leaving you an example, that you should follow in his steps" (1 Peter 2:21).

"We must go through many hardships to enter the kingdom of God" (Acts 14:22).

"Do not be surprised, my brothers, if the world hates you" (1 John 3:13).

"If the world hates you, keep in mind that it hated me [Jesus] first" (John 15:18).

"In fact, everyone who wants to live a godly life in Christ Jesus will be persecuted" (2 Timothy 3:12).

"Consider it pure joy, my brothers, whenever you face trials of many kinds" (James 1:2).

difficult for you to incorporate into your life. What will you do as a result of this study to live a life that reflects these attitudes? Pray for each other before returning to the total group.

6. As a total group, have each man share:
   - One thing that helped me personally in my study of the Season of Suffering is…
   - One thing that spoke to my life in this study of the Season of Success was…

Prayer and Closing Time (5 minutes)

7. Form a circle and have closing sentence prayers starting with the leader. Invite each man to complete this sentence.

   Lord, I praise you for these men because…

CHRISTIAN GROWTH STUDY PLAN

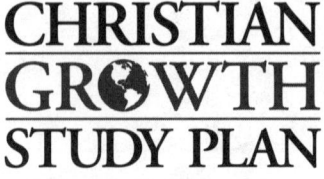

Preparing Christians to Serve

In the **Christian Growth Study Plan (formerly Church Study Course)** this book, *The Seven Seasons of a Man's Life: The Seasons of Suffering and Success,* is a resource in the Christian Growth Category subject area Personal Life. It is also a resource in the Men's Enrichment Diploma Plan. To receive credit, read the book; summarize the chapters; show your work to your pastor, a staff member or church leader; then complete the following information.

Send this completed page to Christian Growth Study Plan; One LifeWay Plaza; Nashville, TN 37234-0117; fax: (615)251-5067; email: *cgspnet@lifeway.com*. For information about the Christian Growth Study Plan, refer to the Christian Growth Study Plan Catalog. It is located online at *www.lifeway.com/cgsp*. If you do not have access to the Internet, contact the Christian Growth Study Plan office (1.800.968.5519) for the specific plan you need for your ministry.